BLOOMSWAY
A DAY IN THE LIFE OF DUBLIN

A Paperback Original
First published 1990 by
Poolbeg Press Ltd.
Knocksedan House,
Swords, Co. Dublin, Ireland

ISBN 1 85371 091 1

Cover design by Peter Knuttel
Illustrations by Peter Knuttel
Typeset by Seton Music Graphics Ltd.,
Bantry, Co. Cork.
Printed by The Guernsey Press Ltd.,
Vale, Guernsey, Channel Islands.

BLOOMSWAY

A DAY IN THE LIFE OF DUBLIN

Desmond Fennell

POOLBEG

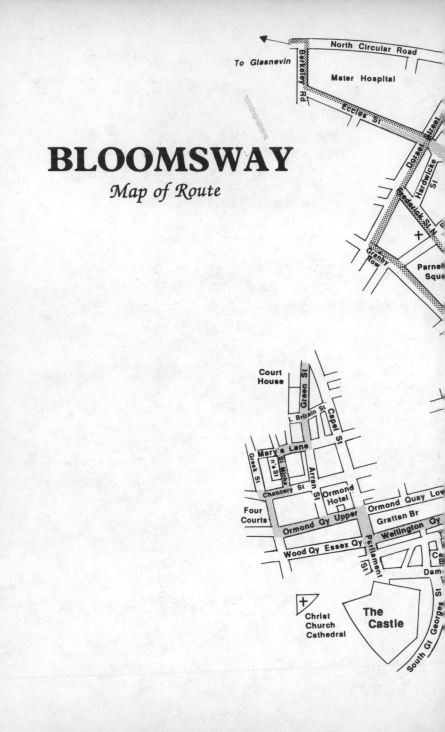

BLOOMSWAY

Map of Route

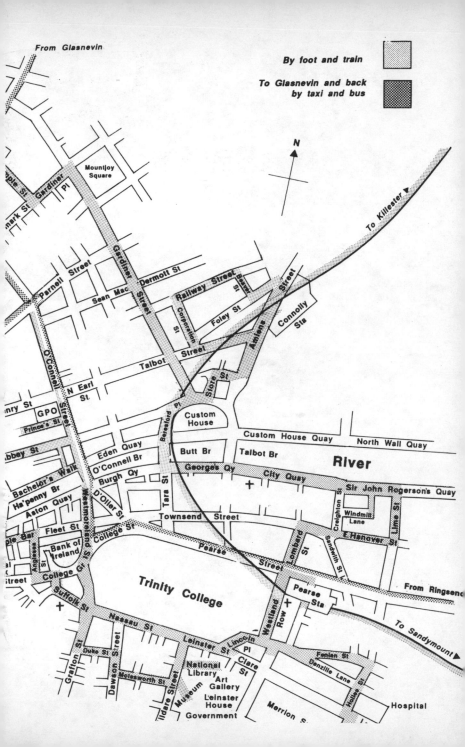

To ML who knows it all

FOREWORD

This is an account of a journey which I made through Dublin on Bloomsday, Thursday 16 June 1988, the year of the Dublin Millennium. I followed the route which Leopold Bloom took in 1904, on the same date and the same weekday—they happened to coincide again. Starting out, as he did, at about 9 am in Eccles Street, and finishing there in the early hours of the following morning, I describe, not his city—*Ulysses* does that, and so do many commentaries—but the Dublin of today.

In several ways, however, I have tried to be helpful to other followers of Bloom. On my journey I kept roughly to the timings of his day. Insofar as the buildings which he visited, passed or noted still exist, I mention them. Where they have been replaced by new ones or by empty spaces, I usually signal this either by not mentioning them or by saying "where such and such once stood" or the like. Out of respect, moreover, for the day it was, I do many of the things that Bloom did, such as buying a newspaper and lemon soap, having lunch in Davy Byrne's, eating in the Ormond Hotel, drinking when, and if possible where, Bloom drank, and "disappearing" in Sandymount for over two hours after six o'clock in the evening. In some instances, of course, it is impossible now to spend parts of the day as he did—to have a bath on South Leinster Street, drink in Barney Kiernan's pub or visit a brothel in Railway Street—and on such occasions I simply found other agreeable ways of passing the requisite time in the appropriate vicinity. Readers acquainted with *Ulysses* will notice these divergences, and regard my substitutes as—I write as a Dubliner—informed suggestions, should they undertake a similar Dublin odyssey themselves.

When Bloom used transport, so did I, but whereas he travelled by trams, carriages or trains, I used buses, taxis and trains in a roughly equivalent pattern, but with inevitable divergences: for example, the bus routes differ from the old tram routes, and a taxi—especially on the long journey to Glasnevin Cemetery—must make some detours to avoid one-way streets.

But the route and some of its incidents are all that I shared with Bloom. It was I who made this journey, not he, and today's Dublin, which is my theme, is in many ways not the Dublin of 1904.

I found Robert Nicholson's *The Ulysses Guide* very useful, and I am grateful to Éamonn Mac Thomáis and Seán Rothery for their advice on some matters.

CONTENTS

9.00 AM - 9.45

ECCLES STREET TO CITY QUAY

It is nine o'clock on the morning of Bloomsday, June 16, 1988, the year of the Dublin Millennium. A Thursday as in *Ulysses*. It is a grey morning, and I am wearing a raincoat just in case. This is the Northside, where I grew up, but that was a few miles away in Clontarf. Living for years now on the Southside, I experience this as strange territory, a different sort of city. Eccles Street is a short distance from the central city area, if you reckon that as stretching from Findlater's Church to Christchurch, the National Concert Hall, Lower Mount Street and the Custom House. Cardinal Cullen and Isaac Butt lived here, and Francis Johnston, Ireland's greatest architect after the Englishman, Gandon, built a few of the houses in the 1750s and lived in No. 64. Until the 70s "Eccles Street" meant for most Dubliners a well-known convent school. When I was a boy at Belvedere College, a few streets away, it was the unofficial "sister" school, from which boys met girls after school hours. But it is gone now. All the houses on that side of the street, from the old Mater Hospital buildings at the top down to the corner with Dorset Street, have been demolished, and they have been replaced only at the bottom by the new Mater Private Hospital. In between, car-parks, with a gaunt, amputated chunk of the convent school standing in them, and further back those new buildings of the public hospital.

Cars are parked on both sides of the street down to where I am standing, outside No. 76. Graceful, silver-coloured lamp-posts line the footpaths, the lamps hanging from floral traceries. No. 76 is roughly opposite where No. 7 used to be. Now the entrance to the Mater Private Hospital stands there, and that fresh red-brick building extends down to Dorset Street. But the houses on this west side are much the same as those on the other side used to be: three storeys above the ground, blackened red brick, Georgian doorways, a basement with railings around it. Some have black iron balconies at the two windows on the second floor, probably the drawing-room of the original family house. Actually, No. 75 is better to look at because on all the windows it has lace curtains that give it a lived-in look. Nos. 76 and 77 are boarded up and have weeds growing on the steps they share. This lower part of the street was built first, around 1750. An RTE van is parked outside the Private Hospital, some broadcasting people standing near it. Perhaps a few of them are the BBC people who I heard were in town for Bloomsday. They're doing a walk with Éamonn Mac Thomáis, the popular authority on old Dublin. When I spoke to him a few minutes ago, he said, in his broad Dublin accent, and that casual manner which belies his erudition, "I'll have a walk down Gardiner Street and onto O'Connell Street to see how it goes." I, too, am heading for Gardiner Street, but will continue straight beyond it to the Liffey.

I have crossed to the Private Hospital and am walking down to the corner. Ahead of me lies that partly derelict area of Georgian Dublin which was the fashionable residential district in the middle of the eighteenth century, until the Merrion and Fitzwilliam areas of the Southside first vied with it, and then, in the following century, triumphed over it. Dorset Street, with its roaring morning traffic, runs along part of the ancient road from the North of Ireland to the bridge over the Liffey that used to be called Dublin Bridge, just above the Four Courts. Looking across it now, I see past a derelict house into Hardwicke Place, and St George's grey church there with its pillared portico, scaffolding on its sturdy, elegant spire. A Church of Ireland church from the great days, and one of Francis Johnston's masterpieces. The clock on the spire figured in my schooldays. In second year, and I think in sixth, we could see it from our classroom window, and as a heavy class passed slowly, it told the time for those of us who had no watches. At the opposite corner of Eccles Street, the yellow Eccles pub, with James Joyce Lounge in large black letters on white. It is done in that handsome Victorian pub-style which has windows flanked by mock-marble Corinthian colonnettes.

I cross Dorset Street to the red Dorset House in the same style, offering Freshly-made Sandwiches, Soups, Rolls, Homemade Apple Pie and Cream, Coffee, Tea, Snacks, Served All Day. Beneath that, "Fuck off". A plane drones unseen in the grey sky heading for the sea. In front of St George's, a semi-circular piazza extends to modern, four-storey blocks of Corporation flats which continue down the other side of Temple Street. The traffic is moderate here, past the old Children's Hospital and St Philomena's Nursing Home. Are these the nurses' and doctors' cars? Ford, Fiat, Austin, Peugeot, Fiat, Renault, Suzuki, Ford. The flats are well kept. A big trailer lorry stands outside them. "Queensway Furniture Warehouse, Santry Village, Dublin 9. World Leaders, Price Beaters". The flats end in a big empty space surrounded by corrugated iron, perhaps a car-park, where a few young trees suggest permanence. Behind this, revealed by the demolition, I am surprised to see the classrooms building of Belvedere. I know the yard, invisible from here, that it looks down on: I hurried across it mornings I was late; spent breaks and lunch-hours there playing relievio or warring in gangs. Joyce was there for some time, though in my day the Jesuits did not include his books in the glass-fronted press for books by Old Belvederians that stood in the Head's reception parlour. Here a sign at the entrance of a large red-brick building says "St Anthony's Shrine", and a big man emerges from a side-door inside the porch, descends the steps, puts on his bicycle clips, unlocks his bike and cycles off. Putting my head in the door he came out of, I see a statue of the saint surrounded by lights, candles, plants and flowers. St Anthony finds lost things. My mother, after ransacking the house, often prayed to him as a last resort, and sometimes lit a candle before our statue of him.

Where Temple Street ends, Great Denmark Street, coming from the right, meets Gardiner Place extending to the left. A long, fairly well-preserved stretch of Georgian facades, invaded by business signs. Almost filling the far end of Denmark Street, Findlater's Church with its delicate neo-gothic spire, named after the shopkeeper who paid for it. In front and beyond it, the trees on the upper side of Parnell Square. The Hugh Lane Municipal Gallery is there. In school lunch-hours spent in its rooms, eating my sandwiches, and inhaling the heady smell of wax floor-polish, I made my first acquaintance with painting.

Left now along Gardiner Place past the Psychiatric Nurses' Association, the Dublin County Committee of Agriculture and the Dergvale Hotel, Bed and Breakfast. Extending to here from Denmark Street is a cluster of small hotels and B and Bs. I used to wonder why they were here precisely. The hotels, with Barry's being the most prominent, form a special social world which I associate with country people and All-Ireland Finals. Later I realised that the connection was precisely that. Croke Park is not far away, and many country people up for the big matches took to staying in this neighbourhood and going dancing on Parnell Square. The teams used spend the night before in Barry's. "Gardiner Place" was for a few years in the 70s a political name. It meant the Official wing of Sinn Féin—as opposed to the

Provisional wing which was "Kevin Street"—after the party and its related army split in 1970. "Gardiner Place" was Marxist, and that Sinn Féin, some years later, became the Workers' Party, thus depriving this street-name of its brief symbolism. But the headquarters of the Workers' Party is still at No. 30. Well-located for its purpose; labour rules the roost here. Transport Salaried Staffs' Association, Irish Munic-ipal Employees' Trade Union, Government and Public Services Union, Marine, Port and General Workers' Union, Labour Party Headquarters—each occupying a house I pass. Ahead, behind railings, the fine park of Mountjoy Square, proclaiming, with its flowers and trees and seats, as do all the parks and public flower-beds of Dublin, the skills and diligence of the Parks Section of the Corporation. Mountjoy was Luke Gardiner by his other, lordly name. He owned all this, conceived it, had it executed. Along the north side of the square, the unbroken parade of Georgian façades show their full splendour, free of hotel and B and B signs.

Crossing the street to continue down the west side, I meet a traffic warden in his brown and yellow uniform, Maor Tráchta on his peaked cap. Near the corner, on a traffic-lights control box of about double the normal height, so that it reaches my eye level, someone has scrawled "Holy City of Vice". I am entering the "war zone". Towards the lower end of the square the derelict houses look like bombed sites. Filthy lace curtains hang in some of the remaining windows. In a third-storey window, the abandoned office of a political group, "Vote Yes for Divorce on June 26", and a poster with a face of Ronald Reagan and the words "Big Blunder Is Watching You". Weeds and desolation as the square ends. On a low building in the corner of the park, "Leithreas. Public Toilet. A.D. 1943". The last house as the square debouches into Middle Gardiner Street is the Society of St Vincent de Paul, Ozanam House, their furniture store. They, too, surrounded by the poor, are well-located for their purpose.

Extending straight downhill towards the Liffey and the domed Custom House, the broad expanse of Gardiner Street carries a great surge of traffic towards me. Cars, green double-decker buses, lorries, mount the hill like an advancing tank army. This blitzed street is, for over half its length, perhaps the most desolate major street in Dublin. Not decayed, but demolished and abandoned and never put together again. Slums replaced by desert and oases of Corporation housing. Wild nature—trees, grass and weeds growing on derelict sites. Weeds—plants out of place. The greatest wild growths are mauve-coned buddleia, a plant that adorns many gardens and whose seeds the birds scatter. Hoardings urge me to drink Tennent's Lager, buy JVC videos and Kodak film, donate my bone-marrow to needy infants and my money to Trócaire to help the people of Mozambique. Women and girls pull shopping-bags and boxes on wheels. The young men and women walk with a desperate jauntiness. The faces of the old are set in hard looks or in placid acceptance. The little pub on the left, Hill 16, does not, as one might imagine, commemorate a knoll on some bleak battlefield for which thousands died, but recalls famed terraces in Croke Park which are packed with thousands for the great games, and which the Dub supporters monopolise when Dublin is playing. At a lone vegetable shop, Tops in Pops, with a large array of prices written on its window, produce is being unloaded from a silver Nissan truck with mud on its tyres. M. Farrell, Hairdresser, on a dead house. At Parnell Street the lights stop us, and The Combat Zone, that's what the sign says, offers French Kick Boxing, Knockdown Karate and Ladies' Self-Protection. In the distance, beyond the twin lines of cheap shops, fast-food bars and small pubs, Parnell on his monument proclaims to O'Connell Street that "No man has a right to fix the boundary to the march of a nation". In North Cumberland Street there, first turn to the left, on a Saturday morning

6

about a month ago, I came upon the weekly street market and was amazed, brought down to earth. Vans had dumped out piles of crumpled clothes and bed-coverings on the tarmacadam, and people were bent over it, picking up this and that. I thought of how others buy their clothes in scented shops on Grafton Street, less than a mile away. I knew there was difference in the city, but not that much, not as between First World and Third World. Some Chinese were picking through the clothes, but it was not that: most were white Dubliners. Further along, on the ground, were piles of used magazines, a broken lamp, children's dolls—the bits and pieces of life from cleared-out flats or rooms.

The lights change and I cross with a woman whose child in a go-car is encased in a hut of transparent plastic. The filthy Honeypot Bar is, fortunately, dead. Across the street, on a low concrete bunker, in a park with young trees fenced with railings, "IDA's Small Business Centre, Gardiner Street, developed in association with the local Community." Perhaps something is happening there. Beside me, towering buddleias, like triffids on the march, run wild across a vacant space towards the new Corporation houses of notorious Seán MacDermott Street, where the people were very disappointed that the Pope did not come to see them when he visited Dublin. In a tarmacadamed emptiness a few cars are parked randomly. Four youngish women in cardigans and skirts, their hands in their pockets, stand beside a blue car, or lean on it, or walk some distance on either side of it and return. Heavy, slow-moving, chatting, waiting, they embody an easy female togetherness. What are they waiting for? Is it for this young man who enters the space and walks towards them? But he veers off in another direction. Railway Street runs left into what was once the brothel quarter, the famed "Monto", the nighttown of *Ulysses*. Through the broken roof and empty windows of a blue building the sky shows. The Iwosaki School of Karate, Wado-Riyu, Principal Japanese

Master Y. Iwosaki. Áras na Comhdhála, headquarters of the Comhdháil Náisiúnta na Gaeilge, the federation of Gaelic language organisations. Years ago, say when Colonel Eoghan Ó Néill headed it, it was a dynamic and central presence in the nation's life. Now, after years of consumerism and Anglo-American cultural mish-mash, it looks and feels relegated; seems aptly placed there beside the Iwosaki School of Karate. Interesting the names they give girls here: graffiti on a lights-controller read "Edel, Samantha, Alison, Sandy", "Wendy, Janice, Lorraine, Lisa". On a wall across the tarmacadamed space, "IRA OK".

As Lower Gardiner Street approaches Talbot Street, houses again fill both sides, the brick now often less dirty-red than dirty-yellow. Here, and extending beyond Talbot Street, another cluster of small hotels and bed and breakfast places, this time explained by the nearness of Connolly Station. Ryan's Hotel. The Holyhead, Guests, Accommodation. Avondale Bed and Breakfast. What was once Moran's Hotel, on the opposite corner with Talbot Street, and a venue for lively meetings of political fringe groups, is now, it appears from a crude green notice over the delapidated entrance, O'Shea's Lounge Bar. Beneath it I read "Springmount House", but the significance escapes me. Through windows of the four empty storeys, workmen are visible at work. In a ground-floor window, Adult Dance Every Thursday. To the left, filling the end of Talbot Street, Connolly Station, its big clock at 9.25. The oldest of Dublin's railway stations after Westland Row, it is the oldest station building, and a fine one. Daniel O'Connell inaugurated it. Every Christmas until I was eighteen we got on a train there, happily, to go to my grandparents in Belfast. To the right, up ramshackle, trading Talbot Street, and similar North Earl Street, I see a corner of the GPO. Beside me a man on a bicycle is carrying a bucket and ladder. In the old days it was as simple as that: you looked at a man and knew his trade. When I write Connolly

Station, I think "Amiens Street Station". Until the fiftieth anniversary of the Easter Rising, in 1966, when Dublin's principal railway stations were renamed after leaders of the Rising, they were known, like Dublin's Catholic churches, by the names of their streets (or, in the case of Kingsbridge Station, the adjacent bridge). Ironically, given the protestations of Protestantism, only Protestant, or rather, Church of Ireland churches were, and still are, known by saints' names. Officially, of course, the Catholic churches have saints' names, but they are hardly ever used. As for the stations, I still often have to pause and think: is Amiens Street Connolly, and Westland Row Pearse, or vice versa? Traffic roars towards us from Amiens Street, then, halted by the red light, pauses to let Gardiner Street flow again.

This final stretch of Gardiner Street heads straight for the Custom House across the expanse of Beresford Place. That yellow building, formerly a Church of Ireland church, says Department of Social Welfare, Employment Exchange, and delivers the dole to men only. Those two with long hair and pale faces, by the wall, look like poets. Those three very tall, very strong-looking men, jostling out through the door, chatting and laughing, off for a pint, might be dockers. I pass under the elevated railway, the so-called Loop Line, starting on its course from Connolly to Tara Street and Pearse. For many Dubliners it means one thing: the bridge that carries it across the Liffey and spoils the view of the Custom House from upriver. *The Irish Catholic*. It used to be, many years ago, on Middle Abbey Street, where the *Irish Independent* entrance is now. A weekly which I see occasionally on sale in Catholic churches, it hardly impinges on public life. Since the *Catholic Standard*, which died in the 60s, Ireland hasn't had a Catholic newspaper that matters nor even a current affairs periodical to equal the British *Tablet*. Some say that is because the ordinary newspapers carry so much Catholic news.

By traffic islands I cross Beresford Place to the Custom House railings and continue along them under the railway towards Butt Bridge. Looking back, I like the brown brick and brown glass of the Irish Life Assurance Centre, like a modernistic palace of the Wizard of Oz. Something to sell that, life assurance. What mankind has sought since the caves. Liberty Hall, at the corner with Eden Quay, all sixteen white storeys of it, the highest building in Dublin, giant in a city of dwarfs where a seven-storey building is unusual. Headquarters still, as in James Connolly's day, of the Irish Transport and General Workers' Union. It was from the old squat Liberty Hall—best-known from the First World War photo that shows "We Serve Neither King Nor Kaiser, but Ireland!" on a banner across the front—that Connolly led his little Citizen Army band to join the Volunteers in the GPO in 1916. The sky, lightening a little, is reflected in the glass all the way up. Across the river, on Burgh Quay, the *Irish Press* building, and towering behind it, with nine or ten storeys, two dull, utilitarian office blocks. The one to the right covers the area where the Theatre Royal stood until the early 60s. It seated three thousand, gave a stage show and a film for the one ticket, and had a troupe of high-kicking dancing girls, the Royalettes, who have had no successors. To the left of the *Irish Press*, the White Horse pub, once the drinking place of its journalists, and then three or four dead houses to Tara Street, directly across the bridge from me.

Standing on Butt Bridge, with heavy traffic flowing northwards, I can see upriver along the bridges to Christ Church and the twin towers of the new City Offices which caused such controversy when a part of the old Viking city was discovered on the excavated site, and conservationists wanted to preserve it. Nothing stirs on the calm water. Since the Guinness barges stopped chugging to and from the brewery upriver, the Liffey is hardly used. Towards the sea, new Talbot Bridge, named after the saintly reformed drunkard, Matt Talbot. It has ejected ships from these quays, as two centuries ago O'Connell Bridge, in collusion with the new Custom House, ejected them from the quays upriver where the old Custom House had stood. Beyond Talbot Bridge, the even newer East Link bridge, which opens to allow ships through. Between them, I see one ship, and there are a few cranes on the south bank, but the cranes clustered on both banks beyond the East Link bridge show that the port really begins there now. Out in the bay to the south side, opposite Ringsend and Sandymount, a plume of white smoke hovers above the two tall chimneys of the Poolbeg power station on the harbour's South Wall. Their height and their red and white bands give them an ethereal quality. I must pause to recollect that it is called Poolbeg power station. The Pigeon House, which had the same function, stood there in my boyhood and for years before that. Much nearer, on the south quays, the tall, white gasometer, which purists call the gasholder. The Custom House, covered in scaffolding, is getting a facelift, perhaps for the Millennium. Two big blue-painted hoardings, suspended on the scaffolding, show architect's elevations of Gandon's masterpiece, paints and palette, architect's instruments. The painter Bobby Ballagh organised a group of unemployed young people to paint them, as a Social Employment Scheme. Just beyond it, behind fences, the Custom House Quay Project is getting under way. Most of the talk has been about its Financial Centre, for which, if one is to believe the papers, Americans, Japanese and British are queuing. But it will also have everything else a yuppie could dream of: luxury flats, a shopping centre, exhibition halls, a marina. With it, the city-centre will continue its historic march eastwards towards the sea, and that might wake up this coastal city to a consciousness of the sea. Although its suburbs stretch around the wide bay, its hustling, bustling and decision-making centre never sees the sea, and has always in my lifetime had the feeling and discourse of an inland city. Indeed, you may well search in Dublin and its environs for a drinking or eating place with a *view* of the sea or even of the river. Since Dublin is the dominating capital of a very centralised island country, this may be one reason why Ireland's performance in maritime matters has in modern times been so paltry. But on second thoughts, considering London up the Thames, Oslo deep inside its fjord, and the maritime prowess of England and Norway, that would be a poor reason. No, what matters, if there is anything in the idea, is the conjunction of the city's centres of power with *ships*, and this has been decreasing; for as the city-centre has moved seawards, bridge after bridge has been pushing the ships ahead of it faster; or rather, for this is the point, out of sight of its power centres. Put the Dáil in the Custom House Quay Project and see the change! Centuries ago, when the centre of Dublin was further upriver, and its city council met, its merchants lived, and the centre of Ireland's administration (the Castle) stood, within yards of ships anchored in the river, then Dublin was an enterprising maritime city, and Ireland had a maritime consciousness. Later, Dublin and Ireland developed an indifference to transport by water. Beneath me, and for miles upstream, flows a boatless, bargeless Liffey.

In the front of the traffic stopped in Tara Street, a green An Post van, a white van and a Bord Telecom orange car, present a casual Tricolour. "Action Hire" on the white van triggers James Bondian imaginings.

I turn left along George's Quay to follow a circuitous route to Westland Row. Late commuters are pouring out of Tara Street DART station. D-A-R-T, Dublin Area Rapid Transit. Beyond the station, on cleared ground, a huge car-park— what's the logic, haven't they DART?—and parked in front of it one of the private buses that commutes for low fares to

Galway. In recent years these private long-distance bus companies, operating on the edge of the law, have been a boon to travellers, but especially to the thousands from the provinces who work in Dublin and wish to return home at weekends. In the long run they forced sluggish, state-run CIE to lower its bus and train fares. Across the river, a full side and rear view of CIE's central bus station, Busáras, Dublin's first experience back in the 50s of the new architecture of glass. To the right of it the sky shows through one of Connolly Station's belfry-like, Italianate towers. A good stone's throw away, in the Custom House Quay Project, a graceful ballet is in progress as a white crane and a brown crane pirouette in opposite directions beside a very tall, slender green crane standing motionless. On Talbot Bridge, a plaque in Irish: Droichead Cuimhneacháin Talbóid was opened in 1978. On the East Link bridge, where you pay a toll, the traffic is light. From the quayside I cross to the footpath at David King and Co. Plumbing Ironmongery. This is City Quay. The buildings, most of them of ordinary house-size, fall into one or other of five categories: dead, half-dead (only the ground floor functions), lopped (the upper part has disappeared), removed (only the ghost haunts the empty space), or, rarely, fully alive, where the entire building is being used for something. City Quay Catholic church—the first Catholic church this morning. When Yves Person, my dear deceased friend from Paris, arrived in Dublin, he visited the two Church of Ireland cathedrals, Christ Church and St Patrick's, on his first afternoon. That evening when I met him, and walked with him through central streets past St Andrew's (on the street of that name) and St Ann's, mentioning that they were Protestant, he exclaimed, "But isn't this a Catholic city? I haven't seen a Catholic church yet." The few Catholic churches in the central city area were built in the days of the Penal Laws or shortly after, and they are located discreetly, so to speak, away from the main street-fronts. Over the entrance to City Quay church, a mosaic Virgin and cherubs. Glancing inside, I recognise it as unreformed, pre-Vatican Two—altars, statues, Lourdes grotto, untouched by the new puritanism. It has the look of a working-class, democratic church, run for and by its people.

Goldcross Wholesale Seed Merchants. In Nelson's, newsagent, I buy the *Irish Independent*, the successor in a sense of the *Freeman's Journal* which it absorbed in the 1920s. The ship I saw moored from Butt Bridge turns out to be a Guinness boat, the blue and yellow *Lady Patricia*, with a sunk, squat funnel. Just after it, among young trees, the City Quay Corporation estate begins. I think it was the second, after the Coombe, of the new, handsome Corporation estates that caused surprise and admiration in the mid-70s. Terraced two-storey houses with steps and basement flats; browns, reds, yellows and green. It extends along the quay across the end of a street and partly up it. But the street has no name-sign and my map does not show the estate. It shows an old street, too small for its name to be written, connecting with the quay here. Through it by way of Lombard Street is the straight route to Westland Row. "What's the name of this street?" I ask a boy, and he says, "I don't know, we're only living here a few weeks". I ask a woman crossing, and she points to a sign on a terrace of houses saying "Robertson's Court", and tells me another terrace is, I think, "Dowling's Court". "But the street itself?" I say, "Or what used it to be?" and she says she'll tell me in a minute, and asks the boy who has been living there only a few weeks. I thank her, saying it isn't important. The rootlessness of new estates. But then a man passing in a blue Toyota van calls out to a woman in a denim suit, "D'you want a lift?" and her face lights up and she jumps in. There are some connections. Across the river the Isle of Man Car-Ferry shed, green and bright yellow, has warehouses behind it, and there are more warehouses downriver from it, salmon-pink and pale yellow, in front of the red-brick building of the British and Irish Steam Packet Company. The B & I ships for Holyhead now leave from far out, beyond the East Link Bridge. I cross Creighton Street to Sir John Rogerson's quay.

SIR JOHN ROGERSON'S QUAY
TO IRISHTOWN

Cé Sir Seán Mac Ruairi, to quote the upper name on the street-sign, begins with a dead house followed by Dix Transport, which no longer transports, but where some workmen are beginning a conversion, one of them tells me, into "some sort of showrooms". Standing precariously on the road amid the speeding cars and lumbering lorries, I look along the first block as far as the corner house with Windmill Lane and count four dead, two half-dead, and one, Dix, showing signs of resurrection. Faded letters on one of the dead buildings say Catholic Seamen's Institute. Even the two "live" ground floors are closed at present. Docker's pub probably opened at 7.30 as the pubs around the docks do, and is closed pending re-opening. The other, with the poster of Nelson Mandela, The Struggle Is My Life, in the window, is the local office of the Workers' Party. Above it, faded curtains hang on windows through which people taking Luncheons and Teas—the words are just legible—once, long ago, looked out on a busy river. Windmill Lane is a magic name in the world of pop and rock, made more magical still since the triumph of U2. Already at its corner, the bright yellow building housing the Riverside Centre for conferences and exhibitions, and Display Contractors Ltd, evokes a change of mood. There are cars parked down the Lane to its L-turn, where I can just see the beginning of the famous U2 Wall.

Opel, BMW, Mitsubishi, Renault, Volkswagen, Citroen, Toyota. I like the way the bright-new Riverside Centre, extending to the L-turn, incorporates the old stone of warehouses. The Wall is covered with inscriptions of U2 fans, in many colours. It runs, I reckon, for over fifty yards along the street and into the courtyard of Windmill Studios. "Love from Norway". "Terry Flanagan, hard man from Manchester". "Bono, tá mé i ngrá leat. You give me the strength I need to carry on. Thank you, Brian". "This wall is available in paperback £5.99 from Eason's". "Please come back to Wales, Love, Gwenllian". "Thanks for the best music in the world, Love, Helen." "Edge, remember two girls backstage Croker, we followed you". "F and G Cassia, Love and thanks for making a stadium feel like the Paradiso in Amsterdam". "U2 you make the best music all over the world, Klaus". "Llegué, no ví y perdí el bus". "Come back to Salt Lake City". "Thank you so much for the two Munich concerts. Remember the mongoloids in the first row. Nadia, Anne". "Adam, please be mine". "Gente irlandesa e quella italiana hanno lo spirito vicino". "Soul, love, this love won't let me go, I love you U2. Robert, Charlotte NC, USA. "Don't forget Newcastle-upon-Tyne in your next tour." I am struck by the classic religious nature of the inscriptions—thanks, devotion, love, petition, as at a sacred shrine. In the yard, about thirty parked cars. Windmill Lane Pictures across from me. Here again the new uses the old stone walls. Helmeted couriers on motorbikes come and go. Smooth young men with slender briefcases cross the yard or dismount from cars.

I regain the quay past Richardson's Tiles which flanks the other side of Windmill Lane, and see the gasometer looming two hundred yards ahead. Birds of a feather flock together: above the closed Waterfront Restaurant, the offices of Upfront Management, Clannad Music, Green Apple Productions, and the film company, Strongbow, which in *Eat the Peach* made the only Irish feature film of recent years that was neither arty nor boring. A truck passes carrying a giant digger-scoop, then a lorry pulling two tiers of cars.

As I turn away from the river up bleak Lime Street, the gasometer follows me like a moon through gaps, and the Nineteen-Eighty-Fourish central stores building of the Electricity Supply Board lours ahead. Beyond it I descry, crossing Upper Erne Street by a bridge, my old friend the railway, Pearse Station now behind it—or in front of it of course, but I am imagining it travelling from Connolly. Wild growths have pushed their way through this high stone wall beside me. On a rusty drainpipe running down it, "Sex is bad for 1, good for 2". Looking through a narrow, barred gate, I see an expanse of green, buddleian wilderness undisturbed for years by man.

Right along East Hanover Street, smelling coffee from Bewley's warehouse on the corner. So this is where the fragrance on Grafton Street originates! I am walking parallel with an oppressive complex of Corporation flats whose three dirty concrete storeys above the brick ground-floor make you notice with surprise the clean lace curtains. They constitute, it appears from a sign, Pearse House, Teach Mac Piarais. Past a scrapyard and Avis Car Rentals, and back across Creighton into Townsend Street, where a triangle opens out, its base formed by the front of the Pearse House complex. I know it is the front because there is a squat tower of red-brick flats standing out from the concrete mass, and an empty flagpole, a tall and massive television aerial, and a high iron gate— with a tree growing directly behind it, barring it. Doubtless it was a solemn scene of civic triumph on the day of its official opening: "Independent Ireland, won for us by men like Pearse, replaces its teeming slums with habitations fit for humans." Past Tipperary Rent-a-Car and Huet Motors I find myself behind the new housing-estate on City Quay, and turn left into Lombard Street at the granite Windjammer pub.

Acme Gerrard Strapping and Stretch Wrapping Systems discomfits me. Joyce House, spick and span in new red brick, announces itself as the Superintendent Registrar's Office for Dublin City and County, Births, Deaths, Marriages. A variation on the usual order, it makes marriage seem an event of the afterlife. Across the street, a bright well-kept block of Corporation flats with newly painted railings and windows. Frank Feely, the City Manager, told me once that it all depends in the end on the people, but Corporation paint does help. Three blue overalled workmen on a balcony recall that group of women in Gardiner Street. One of them is working, two lean contemplatively on the balcony wall, and they are engaged in easy chat. Here it is male togetherness. Above Celsius House—Visit the Window Wonderland—the Lombard Studios theatre where I saw Olwen Fouere the second time in Aidan Matthews' *Diamond Body*. I want to go up Westland Row on the right-hand side, so I cross at Nichols, Funeral Director and Car Hire, reach the corner with Pearse Street and stand waiting for a pause in the traffic. Up Westland Row the delicate iron tracery of the bridge carrying the railway into Pearse Station. Beyond the bridge the grey façade of Westland Row church (properly, St Andrew's), peaking in a statue of the saint with brandished scroll, or is it a cross? A reserved, triumphal Roman baroque. Just across from me, beyond a walled space, an interesting building with much glass is going up. While I speculate on what it might be, the resolute traffic on this one-way artery to the city-centre seems to be giving me no respite, and I see now that the ordained crossing is from the other corner of Lombard Street. So I recross to there, reach the left-hand footpath of Westland Row and cross to the right-hand one. Here, where the walled space is, the Belfast and Oriental Tea Company used to be. The interesting new building is the O'Reilly Institute for Communication and Technology. Now I remember reading that Tony O'Reilly of the fabled wealth and the transatlantic business empire had donated it to Trinity College. Trinity owns most or all of the houses on this side of Westland Row.

Just beyond the railway bridge I cross to a newsagent's, and then, returning down the street past the DART entrance, a green pillar-box and two grey-and-blue metal telephone boxes, I regain the corner with Pearse Street, turn right along it and, after a short distance, right again into South Cumberland Street, to pass through the long gloom beneath the station and emerge near the rear of Westland Row church. The back door is closed, but I follow a black-coated woman with a shopping-bag along a lane connecting with Westland Row and into the church by the side-door. A man's resonating voice is saying "Praise may we give to you and glory". Passing from the chapel where I have entered into the main church building, I see the priest at the altar raising the chalice. It must be ten o'clock Mass. I am standing in a transept, viewing the altar from the side—a post-Vatican Two plain table-altar. Now it's the Our Father, which the congregation recites with the priest. A circle of lights around the head of the statue of the Virgin in the transept opposite. I married there, a quiet wedding such as Westland Row provides. A picture in the paper with Mary and then people knew. "Deliver us Lord from every evil and grant us peace in our day. In your mercy keep us free from sin and protect us from all anxiety, as we wait in joyful hope for the coming of our Saviour, Jesus Christ. Lord Jesus Christ, you said to your apostles, my peace I give you. Look not on our sins but on the faith of your Church, and grant us the peace and unity of your kingdom so that we may live forever and ever." I'll light a candle, as I promised, for my daughter Sorcha who is beginning her Leaving exam in Galway, and for Kate there, too, in the middle of her Inter. Little electric lights are burning on a stand under the statue of St Joseph near me, and other lights are waiting to be lit. They will do, but what must you do to light one? I see, you press a switch and it goes on, it's amazing. The bulb's lit. There must be a place to put money in, but I can't see it, so I leave 10p on the stand, and, as the people go up to Communion, walk down past the confessionals to the back of the church. Over the main altar, in great Roman letters, *ECCE TABERNACULUM DEI CUM HOMINIBUS*. There are about forty people in the church. Old men are sitting quietly at the back; home from home, a stop at the start of their day, with God for a while.

Exiting onto Westland Row, and turning left, I notice, on the far side, how pristine and well-kept Trinity's line of Georgian houses looks. Much as they looked, say, eighty years ago; hardly an intrusion of today's city, no wires, only a couple of traffic signs. The house where Oscar Wilde was born. Once again I think what a mistake UCD made by leaving its old site, and going out to Belfield, instead of expanding around itself on Earlsfort Terrace. Here's Tony Sweeny.

—Would you believe it, he says, I phoned you an hour ago. You must have left early.

—I did, I say, I felt like an early morning walk.

—I wanted to ask you, he says, about another of those mottos in Irish. I don't think it's right in the book. It's the O'Sullivan one.

Tony makes Irish family crests for American tourists.

—Any time, I say. Maybe tomorrow morning? Is it going to rain?

—I wouldn't say so, it's brightening up already. It had better not rain this evening. I'm having a barbecue for the cast of *Desert Song*. I see you've got the paper there. Could I have it a minute to look up when sunset is?

I hand him the *Independent* and he searches through it, not familiar with it.

—9.56. Thanks. Enjoying your walk?

I say I am, very much, and he goes off with a wave. On a step near the Modern Languages shop a tramp sits smoking happily. At the corner with Lincoln Place, I cross to Sweny's the chemist to buy lemon soap. The woman behind the counter says I am the third one asking for it today. It's available in different wrappings, and I choose one in white paper veined with green. She says it is made in England. She had tried around with various Irish firms but couldn't get any of them to come up with the right thing. "You're Mr Fennell, aren't you?" she says, and when I, feeling unmasked, admit it, adds, "I thought so. Have a good day."

Right now past the back-gate of Trinity, the porter in his cabin checking cars, and the Dental Hospital stirring childhood memories of pulled teeth. It's amazing, there are three small cafés now on Lincoln Place, but I suppose they are simply filling the vacuum left by the disappearance of Johnston, Mooney and O'Brien's big coffee-house from South Leinster Street—one of five big coffee-houses, at my reckoning, which have gone from the south city-centre since the 60s. This is where I missed death, by seconds perhaps, on May seventeenth, 1974, when a car-bomb exploded in South Leinster Street in the evening rush-hour. It was during the loyalist workers' strike in the North; the biggest bombing of Dublin since the Northern war began. The unearthly noise I heard ahead of me was one of three bombs that exploded in the city-centre within minutes of each other, killing 23 people immediately—others died later. Most of them were women. When I finally had the courage to turn the corner, it was black chaos, broken windows, hell let loose. There was a charred body near the burned-out car, one of the two people who were killed there. Across from me now as I reach the continuum of Clare Street/South Leinster Street, "P. K. Joyce Demolition Excavation". The sign is on the building which Mr Joyce is knocking down.

Turning right past Bernardo's, one of the few city-centre restaurants surviving from the 60s, and the Lincoln Inn where the Trinity students forbid you a quiet drink, I cross Leinster Street to the new office buildings, stop outside Coyle Hamilton Insurance Brokers, and look back. The last house of the terrace opposite, before the Trinity railings, is Finn's, newsagent and fruit-shop, and high on the gable of the four-storey house, in faded lettering on the red brick, almost hidden by a tall sycamore are the words FINN'S HOTEL. I had been told to look for them. So that's where Nora Barnacle worked; and Joyce first spoke to her on Nassau Street, a few paces away, and their first *rendezvous*, which she missed, was just over there beyond Clare Street, on the corner of Merrion Square, outside the house the Wildes moved to.

It is ten-thirty, I need a coffee, and I want to make a phonecall, so I make for the Livingroom on Lincoln Place, sit at a table in the jutting window with a direct view of the street, open my *Independent*, and light my pipe. When I was getting my coffee at the counter, the girl was talking with a friend about the new Anna Livia fountain on O'Connell Street which has been donated to the city by Michael Smurfit, the other Irishman of fabled wealth who has a transatlantic business empire. I have not seen it yet, but I have read that it's a bronze reclining woman with water cascading over her, and that it is to be opened, if that's the word, this afternoon. The friend, another girl, said:

—There's a fence around it, y'know, but y'can go in and look. She's a green, skinny wan, sittin in a bath like, with the water bubblin all round her. D'y'know what they're callin her?"

—No, said the coffee girl, what?

—The floosie in the jacuzzi—isn't that brilliant?

—What's a jacuzzi? said the coffee-girl.

—Y'mean a say y'never heard of a jacuzzi? It's a bath that keeps bubblin all round y'and two can sit in it.

— Sorta handy, said the coffee-girl and grinned.

The headline on the front page of the paper, "FUN RUN CARNAGE" is about the six British soldiers who were blown up in their van last night in Lisburn after they had taken part in a mini-marathon. The Irish soccer team is "on course for the semi-finals" of the European Cup after drawing with the Soviet Union in Hanover. The Dáil "unites in a clemency request to British Home Secretary, Douglas Hurd, in the controversial Birmingham Six case". "English disease plagues Germany, Page Eight"—without looking, I know that's about the soccer hooligans. But I do look to see what they mean by saying that on Page Seven, to mark Bloomsday, they "present a tour of the real Joyce country". They mean, it turns out, a tour of the Northside, conducted by Ken Monaghan, a nephew of James; it's "real Joyce country" because the Joyce family lived in ten different houses there. At the bottom of the same page, an article by Bruce Arnold, the literary editor, whom I'll be meeting for lunch, on "the first Bloomsday celebration, back in 1962". On another page a big picture of Ken Monaghan with the painter, Gerald Davis, in bowler hat and with Jewish face doing his Leopold Bloom act. In the Ascot Gold Cup at 3.45 there are thirteen declared runners, with Primitive Rising the favourite at 100/30, Shimsek and Spruce Baby outsiders at 25/1. Sunset, four minutes to ten, at Sandymount Strand. A whole hour and a half later than in 1904. Well, you can't have everything: I must be in Holles Street by then. Gillian Bowler with her beagle on the cover of the "Lifestyles" supplement. The travel agent who sold her business to a British firm for four million. I was at a christening party a month ago in her yellow mews house surrounded by a garden with three ponds and enormous Cretan jars. With the beagle climbing over her, she's laughing, so her mouth is open, but in the three "serious" pictures on an inside page she also has her lips apart, teeth showing. Meryl Streep often poses like that in her films, but without the teeth, just lips open, and once I had noticed it, it struck me as affected, the first and only flaw I had found in her. I have tried holding my lips open like that and it becomes very tiring after a short time. But perhaps it's natural for some people. Gillian seems a natural sort. I use

25

the Livingroom's telephone to call Ronan Sheehan, the young writer, who is doing a book on the Dublin Liberties, and his wife tells me he won't be able to meet me this evening at Holles Street for the last hours of my journey.

It's a quarter to eleven as I leave to return to Westland Row. The buses to Sandymount are away down on Townsend Street and, I'm sure, not to be trusted, so I'll take the DART one stop to Lansdowne Road for Newbridge Avenue. The day is definitely brightening, and getting warm. The tramp is still sitting there. The man in the ticket-office says the trains come every ten minutes and my fare is 65p. I haven't yet seen the turnstiles working in a DART station, and they mustn't be working here today, because a man in CIE uniform is checking the tickets. I ask him for one of the timetables he has beside him in a pile. An escalator takes me up to a wide floor of black and white squares under a high curved roof which is open at both ends to the light and air. Some wan young trees in barrels are pawns on the chessboard. Will CIE think of putting big chess-pieces here so that passengers can make a few moves while waiting for trains? To the left a door says FIR, with GENTLEMEN underneath it, and a door beside it, SEOMRA NA mBAN, LADIES' ROOM. Mounting a few steps I reach the red-tiled platform and can see across the tracks. Some people are sitting on benches. "Worried about your next move? Call the experts, Lisney and Son, Estate Agents." "Pregnant? Worried? Would you like to talk to us about it in confidence? Yes, we can help. Phone CURA now." "Have You Behan to Easons?" "CHILDLINE. For children in trouble or danger. Phone 01 793333 or dial the operator 10 and ask for Freephone Childline. Speak to someone who cares." A picture of a sad little girl. "Turn the tables. Smirnoff Vodka" and a picture showing a handsome young man seated at a table in a public place drinking Smirnoff, and, at the table next to him, a beautiful girl beside another handsome man. The man on his own is looking happily at the girl and she is

returning his look with interest, while the face of the man beside her looks worried and downcast. A large blue metal board suspended perpendicularly over the platform has words along the top: "Next southbound train stops at", and is blank beneath that, though there are some scratches on the blue surface.

Powered by electricity, a green train ambles towards us over Westland Row, stops and opens. Two men and a woman leave it, seven or eight of us board, and straightaway it takes us among backs of houses with the gasometer off to the left, and we have views of the roofs of little houses. The Grand Canal Basin and the silos of the Dock Mill. I seldom use the DART. Mainly it serves the affluent suburbs on the south side of the bay and the similar suburbs at the northern tip. It cost £110 million. That was a few years ago when I was living in the West, and it annoyed me and many others that, while that money was being spent on Dublin which has everything, the Government was refusing £3 million to the Mayo people to finish the airport at Knock, which was to be the first proper airport in Connacht. A white elephant, the Government said, but the Mayo people found the money elsewhere, and Knock airport is making a profit, while DART is not. To the right now, behind Victorian terrace houses, there are old back gardens with walls and trees. And come to think of it, *what* happened in all those intervening years since 1904, when Bloom was able to take a train late at night from Westland Row, miss his stop in Amiens Street, get out at Killester and get a train back in a matter of minutes? That was at 11.30, and I have heard that DART, incredibly, stops running just about that time, when the buses stop. Which is why I must look at this timetable, but I am not good at timetables, and we are slowing down for Lansdowne Road, heading straight for the West Stand of the rugby stadium, and there is a glimpse, just before we pass under its rear buttresses, of the pitch and the aerial leap of the new East

Stand. Then we slide over a level crossing to a halt. Trees rise behind the platform. In less than two minutes from Westland Row we are in a leafy suburb. Following some people I walk along the platform reading "Easons Something to Synge About", towards the sign which says "Ó dheas, Bré"—Bray being the southern terminus—where the knowing ones turn, and I follow, down covered steps, between walls of coloured tiles, and, echoingly, under the tracks, to steps that lead up and onto the other platform, and through a turnstile that turns and into a passage between heavy green iron sheets and railings onto Lansdowne Road, beside the level crossing.

Turning right across it, I am conscious of the West Stand of the rugby stadium looming over me. I am not a rugby man, nor indeed do I go to football matches, but that's what Lansdowne Road means pre-eminently for the world. I am entering Old Sandymount, as it's sometimes called, the newer part being off to the right. The line of numbered, closed entrances to the stadium face a row of pleasant houses with gardens and some trees. From inside the stadium a magnified voice counts from one to ten, seeming to mimic the numbers on the gates. Three tall Lombardy poplars stand against a sky which is showing blue. A plane is passing, pulling a streamer with lettering that I cannot read. The lofty East Stand, like a gigantic concrete thrusting V lying on its side in mid-air, seems a living thing. I like Sandymount, tucked away between the railway and the sea. The fashion for "townhouses" has made it a favourite place to live; near the city-centre and the main road to the southside of the bay, but removed from them, with a life of its own. Sandymount, or by its Gaelic name, *Dumhach Trá*, strand dunes. You can see it marked as tidal sand on the postcard maps of Dublin in the eighteenth century which the Millennium has brought into the shops. To the left, across the river ahead—it must be the Dodder—the two Poolbeg chimneys, with their plume of smoke, tower distantly behind the houses of Newbridge Avenue, and I see a small crowd gathered there. On a bench beside the bridge an old man sits reading his paper. Walking around at this time one sees what retired men do with their mornings.

Left into Newbridge Avenue, and there are ponies and traps and people on this side of the road. They must be preparing for a Bloomsday ride along the funeral route to Glasnevin. Now that I recall, this is one of the special events which the city has got up for the Millennium. On the far side of the street the old houses are mingled with more recent ones, but on this side all are old, with gardens behind low railings. There are several different kinds of horse-vehicle.

—What do you call these? I ask a group of top-hatted jarveys who are chatting together.

— Jaunting-cars, says one.

—Well, yes, I say, but haven't they particular names?

—That's a cabriolet, that's a buggy, and that's a visby, says the same man, and then there's argument about another one.

—A dog-car.

—A travelling car.

—But we call them all jaunting-cars.

The Lord Mayor, Carmencita Hederman, with shining face, enjoying her job. Yes, she says, when I ask her, she knows the people in No. 9. Tom Mitchell, antique dealer. "It's further along on this side." When she is out of earshot, someone says, "She should know, he has often acted as her election agent". No. 9 has its green door standing open, hydrangeas and flowering roses against the wall. A woman comes out and runs towards the crowd. Three men pass on the far side wearing boaters with blue bands. At the end of the Avenue, consulting my map, I decide that the Star of the Sea Church is not the ecclesiastical-looking building immediately over there to the right, but the one further away, with a tree partly hiding it. I am looking for a telephone to call a taxi, and take the left turn towards Irishtown village, where the natives used have their shanty-town beside the sand dunes.

Just past St Matthew's Church of Ireland church there is a phone-box outside Clarke's pub. I look up taxi-ranks in the Directory, phone the rank on Lansdowne Road, and say:

—Glasnevin Cemetery. I'm standing on the footpath in Irishtown, outside Clarke's pub.

—That's not good enough, says the man's voice. How do I know you'll be there when I come?

And the phone goes dead. So I enter Clarke's, phone again, and it's another man.

—I'm in Clarke's pub in Irishtown, I say.

—I'll be right over, says the voice.

I go out and stand in front of the pub, noticing that the date on St Matthew's school across the road is 1904. Was it finished when Bloom passed it? The first carriage of the funeral procession, an empty hearse, is emerging from Newbridge Avenue and coming towards me. Two motorcycle police roar out of the Garda station opposite, wait for the hearse to reach them, and set off in front of it, opening the way. Does that mean they will have special permission to go the wrong way through the one-way streets? To be absolutely and literally authentic? The best I can do in the taxi is skirt close around them. Carmencita is in the first coach.

—Come on in, come on in, a laughing woman beside her in an Edwardian dress and bonnet calls out to me.

All of them pass, the buggies and cabriolets and dog-cars and visbies. Then a vintage car, with a couple sitting in the boot, and more cars behind that. The taxi arrives, four minutes it took, and I set out for Glasnevin along Irishtown Road.

—That fellow before me, did he refuse to come for you? asks the driver.

—Yes, indeed, I answer.

—I heard him, some of them do that. They're not supposed to, you know. They pick and choose.

It is twenty-five past eleven on my watch.

11.25 - 12.40

IRISHTOWN VIA GLASNEVIN TO O'CONNELL STREET

I can see the end of the "funeral" some distance ahead. They are pilgrims really, following in the way of the saint. Convivial, like Chaucer's pilgrims setting out for Canterbury, or like Mac Dara's in Cárna, a month from now to the day, piling into the boats at Mace pier to be ferried to the saint's island and the little church that has become known to the world from Irish postage stamps. This Bloomsday thing is gathering strength from year to year, becoming a secular "saint's day" and a secular pilgrimage. Of course, from the start it was that, privately, for the learned Joyceans, who inaugurated it back in the early 60s—1962 according to Bruce Arnold's article in the *Indo*—when Myles na Gopaleen gathered a few other priests of the cult—Niall Montgomery, John Ryan, Donagh McDonagh, even a priestess, Harriet Weaver—for an expedition in two horse-drawn carriages starting out from the Tower in Sandycove. But in recent years, as its "events" have multiplied, and commerce has shown interest, and the media have played it up, non-devotees have joined in for the fun; it has become almost a civic thing and this year the city officially, even the Lord Mayor, is taking a hand in it. It is very much a pilgrimage when you come to think of it. People journey—some this, some that stretch of the sacred path—and people do prescribed things in prescribed places. On Mac Dara's island they walk around stone graves and circles saying prescribed prayers. They attend Mass at the gable of the little church, listen to the readings, hear a speech in the saint's memory, receive Communion. In Dublin today they look across the Bay from the Tower, or buy lemon soap in Sweny's, or eat pork kidneys for breakfast in certain restaurants. In Davy Byrne's they drink the saint's particular wine, and eat bread with his particular cheese, doing this in commemoration of him. All over the city until the Bloomsday banquet tonight they will be listening to readings from the sacred Book, joining in re-enactments of the sacred Story, and delivering or attending to homilies, sober or well-oiled, suited to the occasion.

Ringsend village, which we are entering, is very recognisable as a place in itself, and in view of its history ought to be. The end of the *Rinn* or headland that jutted through the sand into the rivermouth, this was the place where for centuries ship's passengers disembarked for Dublin. They were transported from here by horse-car to the city upriver. And it was hereabouts that the city's cobblers had their annual holiday outing, the Waxies' Dargle, those strange words made well-known by the old song. First comes this pleasant square of modest, two-storey houses, with a squat, rectangular public library in the middle. The library is surrounded by grass and railings, displays a remarkable, massive doorway in a style that looks Assyrian, and shares an extensive, kerbed island with a group of young trees and a couple of park benches. Swinging sharply to the left around these, past Ringsend Cycle Centre and Carlile Cleaners, we come abruptly, pausing for traffic lights, on a dramatically urban sight in this suburban setting. There is an L of weathered houses, all shops or pubs, well painted by people who know colour, in reds from maroon to pink, yellows from ochre to cream, greens and blues. The upright of the L, our route to the city, reaches towards, and climbs with, a steep humped bridge over the Dodder. To the right of the bridge, and abutting on it, a handsome granite Catholic church with a clock in its tall spire. Framed between the church and the climbing houses, the ridge of the bridge gives onto blue sky with white clouds and, against the sky, at a short distance, the two rectangular grey bulks of Boland's Mill connected by aerial stairways. From a pub a few yards away a man emerges, wiping his mouth, and half-blesses himself towards the church. Down the bridge towards us comes a man with peaked cap, in blue boiler-suit, pushing a hand-cart.

Behind a long line of cars we move over the hump, and descend past the Shelbourne greyhound stadium, where on Monday, Wednesday and Saturday evenings the dog-people, a special breed, parade their sleek, skeletal runners to the starting-point, and breaths are held, for nineteen seconds, thirty seconds or thirty-four, while streaks of four-legged lightning, pursuing the ridiculous, rattling hare, make money and lose it, repeatedly. The intense, quiet women, they strike you most, from office-desk or terraced house you think as you regard them, gaze rigidly while the hounds streak, then look down, mark their cards, and wait contentedly. Another humped bridge lies ahead, and, to the right, old industrial buildings extend towards the docks. Great lorries trundle past. Boland's Mill was garrisoned by the insurgents in 1916. It commanded the railway line into Dublin from Kingstown. But why, I wonder, would the troops have to land there? Couldn't they have come straight into Dublin docks? An aunt, a sister of my father's, told me that he was with the Boland's Mill garrison. But he never spoke to me about it, and I was grown up when she said that. I never asked him what he was doing in Dublin in 1916, though I knew he was there, for a letter she gave me proved it. The mill abuts onto the humped bridge over the Grand Canal Basin, its high, windowed end-wall falling sheer into the still water. Here the canal comes finally to rest from its Midland traverses.

Often when I see it in the city, and now here, those flat grasslands swim into my mind. Beyond the basin, far inland, the Two Rock and Three Rock mountains—which I know, where I have walked and cycled now and then since boyhood—rise gently against the sky. Ahead to the left, behind Ventac The Ventilation Centre, the Dogs' and Cats' Home. Towards the Liffey the white gasometer looms again, friend from earlier, and the riverside cranes are still motionless.

Descending, I see that the tall stone building on the left is the Tower Design Centre which the IDA set up a few years ago in what was once the Hammond Lane Foundry. That means we're in Pearse Street. David Ward, who was a next-door neighbour before he emigrated to Australia with his Croat wife, had a workshop in the Tower for his wooden toys. I'm sorry I never visited him there, for he was the only one I ever knew who worked there, and it is said to be a honeycomb of craft workshops. All those big new buildings around it must be what the IDA calls its Enterprise Centre, "the biggest in Europe". I am impressed. They seem to be serious about their switch from multinationals to encouraging home enterprise; and about time. Sinn Féin. How it annoys me when people mistranslate that as "Ourselves alone"! St Andrew's Resource Centre in the old national school. Pearse Street is a shambles of a street. Hardly a decent set of houses or a decent building in sight, except for the elegant Florentine tower of Tara Street fire-station beyond the railway bridge leading to Westland Row. That great bulk of a building on the left was the Central City Library until they moved it to the Ilac Centre in Henry Street. But it still houses the Gilbert Library of books on Dublin. I looked at Gilbert's own three volumes there. We are leap-frogging past the funeral carriages, have caught up with and passed the hearse. The taxi-driver says the horses are the wrong colour: they should be black. They are brown.

—I recall, he says, when you used see them on the streets in the old days. They were fine horses and they used wear waving black plumes, on their heads, you know.

Through the open window beside him we hear a man, who is standing watching the sight, call out to a woman:

—*There's* something for you! A bit of nostalgia.

She smiles happily and continues to watch—wondering, doubtless, what on earth they are up to.

The lights stop us at the corner of Westland Row. It seems a long time since I crossed here, but it's less than two hours. We move, and there's the Academy Cinema, which before my time was the storied Antient Concert Rooms, and which now leads a sporadic, non-musical existence. The last time I visited it, dutifully—one must support Irish films—was to see Cathal Black's boring films about the Christian Brothers and about a houseful of loony Dublin down-and-outs and squatters. Full of bilious anger the one, full of Significance and Social Concern the other. St Mark's old church behind its garden.

—We'll go through Westmoreland Street and O'Connell Street, I say to the driver.

—That's not the way to Glasnevin, he says. We should go through Tara Street.

—I have a special reason.

—As you say, he answers, not happy.

Allied Carpets was Patrick Pearse's house. Willie's too, the family home. The brothers' profiles are too high on the wall for me to see them. Opposite the fire-station, probably where that tax office, Áras an Phiarsaigh, is now, was the Queen's Theatre. I saw a pantomime there as a child, and I was at a play or two when it housed the Abbey after the old Abbey was burnt down. Moving between the Trinity College wall on the left and the palatial police-station we come to Cliodna Cussen's stone pillar which commemorates and replaces what the Vikings called the "Long Stone". It doesn't give much chance for Cliodna to show her talent. I like her work, when she sculpts. Through D'Olier Street there is a glimpse of O'Connell Bridge and the beginning of O'Connell Street. But to get there we must go around by Westmoreland Street, turning at Tom Moore's statue opposite the Bank of Ireland. I feel the driver's annoyance. This is not the proper route.

I recall the sense of a poem from the 50s or 60s, by Tom Kinsella perhaps or Val Iremonger, about a saint's day. There was this saint, long ago, who fasted and tortured himself and prayed long hours, a hermit. Now, on the spot where he lived and built his chapel, behold the people disporting themselves, the laughter and the dancing. Out of that came this. Not very apt really, since Bloom did not fast or torture himself or pray. But he has produced the same result. Or rather, the fiction of him has. All the saints who are celebrated by saint's days are ghosts, but he is the most ghostly of ghosts since he was a fiction to begin with. *The Invention of Tradition*, the book that showed how, towards the end of the last century and the beginning of this, the middle classes throughout Europe invented traditions, so that what seemed and was called "traditional" as I grew up was often in fact no older than that. Santa Lucia in Sweden, German student fraternities, patterns at holy wells in Ireland which the Gaelic League and other revivalists started. Reactions against the mass uprooting called modernisation, and its cult of novelty, they were novelties themselves, or inno-vations rather, made into affirmations of the past and expressions of continuity. Bloomsday is a recent instance, a small fight-back against the latest wave of modernisation that swept over us in the 60s.

For the Millennium they are widening the tree-lined is-lands that run down the middle of O'Connell Street. This confines the wheeled traffic even more than before into two "streets" on either side. The talk has been of making the centre a proper promenade, under trees, from O'Connell's statue past all the others to Parnell's. But I cannot see how that will succeed unless they actually join up all the islands and eliminate crossing traffic, and I doubt they will do that. So it will be a half-measure, and the likely outcome is that a wide central stretch of the street will remain largely deserted. Long Millennium banners are hanging down the pillars of the GPO: Baile Átha Cliath A Thousand Years. But the Millennium has not managed to replace Nelson's Pillar, though there has been a great deal of talk about it. There has been talk about it for years, but there is a difficulty, a dilemma. With O'Connell at one end of the street, Parnell at the other, and the empty Pillar space in front of the GPO over which the Tricolour flies daily to honour the 1916 Rising, it is pretty obvious that a monument to Pearse, Connolly, or both of them, or something on those lines, should be there. People know this, and some years ago there was a push which I joined in to put Connolly there. But we have become confused about our history and our fight for independence, and some important people are embarrassed and apologetic about it, so that the obvious has become controversial and there is paralysis, our old familiar, which Joyce remarked on and Wolfe Tone before him. Instead, just north of the Space—just beyond McDowell's The Happy Ring House— we are getting Smurfit's Anna Livia fountain which the girl called the floosie in the jacuzzi. The fence is still up around it. Will it be ready for opening this afternoon? Among the trees, Father Mathew's little statue, its left hand uplifted, is the smallest in the street. You could forget it's there. At the end of the taxi-rank opposite the Gresham Hotel, the Sacred Heart, with both arms uplifted, is in his glass case with flowers. At the Parnell monument we stop. His right arm is extended sideways, the hand slightly above shoulder level, his utterance about the march of the nation in golden letters beneath him. The Ambassador Cinema is showing *Wall Street*.

A sort of marginalised Cinderella among the city-centre cinemas, it fits unhappily into its grandiose rotunda building. I say rotunda with emphasis, for clearly, as anyone can see from the ornate, semi-circular roof, the Ambassador building together with the Gate Theatre behind it, and not the Hospital so-called, is, or rather contains, the Rotunda. To get to Dorset Street we must turn left here and go around two sides of Parnell Square.

This well-used, history-laden square is not elegant like the other great squares, and it is different from them in that its most notable buildings are *in* the square, not around it. It was the pleasure centre of the fashionable Northside in the eighteenth century, after Dr Mosse had built his maternity hospital—which we *call* the Rotunda, despite its tower and rectangular shape—and the concert hall, assembly rooms and gardens which raised funds for it. The concert-hall and assembly rooms were in the Rotunda proper, and that has seen history. The Patriot Volunteers in Grattan's day met there, and the Irish Volunteers were founded there. The Gate, under Mícheál Mac Liammóir, Hilton Edwards and Lord Longford, rivalled the Abbey, and it has lately been having a renaissance, with reassuring, chocolate-box theatre for the bourgeoisie, since Michael Colgan took over its management. But the houses around the square, or many of them, gave it another flavour in my student days and later. The Gaelic League and Sinn Féin a few doors from each other on the east side; Coláiste Mhuire, the all-Irish school, a stone's throw away; the dance-halls, National and Ierne and the Irish Club, where the "real people of Ireland", city-dwellers from the country and their country cousins when in town, danced old-time waltzes and foxtrots to the big bands and the country bands and listened to the singers of country music—all this made it the Irish-Ireland square. When the big Gaelic matches brought the countrypeople to town there was a great confluence flowing from Croke Park through Gardiner Place and Denmark Street—a carnival of nationalism. The Garden of Remembrance came to cap this in 1966. But by then this Green ethos was already on the wane. Sinn Féin had long gone elsewhere and the Gaelic League had just departed. Dancing fashions were changing. But as we turn up the west side, there is *An Phoblacht*, the Provos' paper, and after Desmond Domican's Academy, Ballet, Speech and Drama, Sinn Féin back again, but looking fortified against assailants. Domican, that uncomfortable, much-mocked fat boy in my class at school, whom we thought a cissy, had his gift and his niche in life. The sign Disco Disco has a yellow sun above the words, and beneath them, a green palm-tree and a yellow mound suggesting sandy desert. Why, now, should a tropical desert island suggest disco-dancing on Parnell Square? Because, I suppose, the desert island is "escape", and dancing in the dark to flashing lights and deafening music offers that, and is that.

Between trades union offices and Coláiste Mhuire, Pro Deo Pro Patria, we pass into Granby Row. In that lane, with St Saviour's church at the end of it, Matt Talbot, he of the new bridge, died. "Rev. Austin Flannery OP, St Saviour's, Dominick St", I wrote on many an envelope, sending articles to that great editor and loyal friend. Years ago; our ways have parted. A pub, The Waxies' Dargle. Why here? *Can* it be because of the National Wax Museum opposite, Children's World of Fairytale and Fantasy? Like the pub in Frenchpark, Co. Roscommon, near Douglas Hyde's birthplace and grave, called The Hyde Out. God help us!

The Black Church, ahead of us, juts its jagged teeth sky-wards as we turn right and are back in bustling Dorset Street, the great north road. We have climbed from Parnell Square, and ahead the road is rising again. The Northside. Why did the Southside woman marry the Northside man? To get her handbag back. What is a Northsider in a three-roomed house?

A burglar. In a suit? A bus conductor. On the Southside the Northsider has replaced the Kerryman.

The Bloomsday thing fulfils the need for pilgrimage for people who would never dream of doing a real pilgrimage. That, too, tallies with the 60s which brought a sharp new blast of secularisation to a city already remarkably secularised. A Catholic city which, unlike so many Catholic and post-Catholic cities, has no pilgrimage, nor indeed any public processional or theatrical manifestation of religion. In Bonn on St Martin's Day, the thousands of singing children walking with lanterns at dusk in the streets, all the church bells tolling. The Passion processions of Seville, the *Virgen* this and *Virgen* that carried through every Spanish city. The sumptuous civic Corpus Christis. The *presepes* everywhere in Rome at Christmas; even in the Termini station, with music, and little shepherd's fires burning. Of course a local pilgrimage or pattern like Mac Dara's Day, tied to a place where people live, is not just or even principally a religious event. It is a celebration of place and community, and Bloomsday, in its naive, happy way, is that too, for the few who are aware of it.

—Left here please, I say to the driver as we are reaching Eccles Street.

—This is a terrible way round, he says, moving his head and shoulders in physical pain. You have me going all over the place.

—I'm paying you for it.

—Oh you'll pay me for it all right, he says, resentfully.

What's he so angry about? Could it actually be professional pride? Eccles Street continues the climb. The proper name of Glasnevin Cemetery is Prospect Cemetery. Before it was surrounded by houses, it must have commanded a view.

Between the old Mater building and the monument to the Four Masters, we turn right onto Berkeley Road and enter Phibsboro. Two couriers race past us, the names of their firms, Hurricane and *Anois* (Now), emblazoned on their black leather jackets. They are everywhere these days. People marvel at them in their spaceman outfits on their daredevil courses. Obviously they fulfil a need and fill a gap. At the beginning of this century Dublin had six postal deliveries a day; lovers—who else would do it?—could write five letters in one day and get answers to them. Beyond Egan's Wholesalers the twin stone towers of Mountjoy Prison rise ahead against the sky. Lord Mountjoy of the Square and Gardiner Street had plans to be remembered better in these parts. If they'd been realised, there would be no Mater nor Four Masters monument nor Mountjoy jail. A vast Royal Circus, grander and larger than the greatest squares, would have put the Northside on top for good. Instead, there is no conception worth the name, only little streets of little houses any way. And the towers of the 'Joy keeping watch over them.

Left onto the North Circular Road, a grandiose scheme from the grandiose days that was realised before the small-thinkers. We slow to a stop beside a small statue on a pedestal among shrubs. A uniformed guerilla fighter on one knee, rifle at ready, commemorates the deceased members of C Company, First Dublin Brigade of the Army of the Republic. On the low wall a man sits reading a paper. Down a slope behind the statue, a linear stretch of tended grass and trees, with benches at intervals. A spur of the Royal Canal once ran there to Broadstone Station. With Toyota, Toyota and Peugeot around us, we move towards the crossing with Phibsboro Road. Ice Skating, Three Sessions Daily. A girl in short skirt, one leg raised, smiles radiantly at me. At Doyle's Corner, the crossroads, the buildings have a sturdy, civic air. The centre, so to speak, of haphazard Phibsboro. Beyond it, where we must now go to detour, St Peter's great church stands in the junction with Cabra Road. Between the church and the red-brick houses, with only a tree interposing, a great vista of sky towards Cabra and the plains. St

Peter's, St Saviour's—I was wrong, or rather I exaggerated: there are *some* Catholic churches called by their saint's names; usually, for some reason, those that belong to religious orders. What was in my time the older city ends around here. These red-brick houses symbolise it for me subconsciously; I read them that way. Beyond the red brick, Cabra, and the other new suburbs that were built from the 40s on, come to my mind in cream and grey colours, concrete blocks and pebble dash. The sense of exile of the slum-dwellers rehoused there where the awful empty *country* began!

Passing the church, we turn right up St Peter's Road, past No. 7 where the Joyces lived, and by coincidence Stephen Dedalus. Between the terraces of houses, lanes lead into Dalymount Park, spiritual home of Irish soccer, where internationals were played once, but now no more, since the crowds have grown too big for it. Right into Connaught Street and we are back at Phibsboro Road, between Abrakebabra, Magic Food, in the ugly big shopping-centre, and the Corner Wine Specialist, where Mary and I stopped once to look and found retsina at a reasonable price. We used hunt it because it was the drink of our honeymoon.

Left now and we regain the main route. Cross Guns pub takes its name from the bridge ahead of us over the Royal Canal. So does Cross Guns Tyres just beyond the bridge. But there was once a place nearby, Cross Guns, which named the bridge, and perhaps before that an inn which named the place. And before that again there was Daneswell, and earliest of all, Magduma, or in the Icelandic saga, Dumazbakka Bru, the place where Brian Boru was slain in his tent after he had won the battle of Clontarf against the Danes—or the "Danes", as the newest, revised history would write that, for the opposing army were mostly Norwegians with some Gaels. The pub on the left just before the bridge bears his name, and a builder's sign the name of his people. Dalcassian Downs, it announces, has splendid three-bedroomed houses with all mod cons. And in that name come together the ancient history of the place and this latterday Dublin fashion of giving new housing-estates names that sound English. Downs. What is a down? On the down over there. "On the what?" Did the inn sign, supposing there was an inn, show crossed guns to commemorate the battle—using, anachronistically, guns instead of swords? Beyond the bridge, at a flowered triangle, we veer left, pass monumental sculptors on both sides, and are into Finglas Road along the cemetery wall, dark cypresses rising behind it. The houses just before it were called Bengal Terrace in the old days. In the wide space in front of the main gate we stop at seven minutes to twelve. The journey took twenty-nine minutes. He says £6.40 and I pay him in silence.

There are parked cars, taxis delivering people, and other taxis waiting. The living move in both directions through the gate. Inside, in an open, tarmacadamed space, a hearse stands. A slender green lightning conductor runs down O'Connell's round tower. The tower is good to look at. It is one of those happy thoughts which, when executed, seems to have been inevitable, so precisely and splendidly does it serve its purpose and signal the cemetery miles away. In front of it an angel atop a monument is holding a spear, which as I move becomes a cross. Celtic crosses, that noble Irish contribution to graveyard furniture, stand crowded, forest-like, to the right, interspersed with statues. On the coffin in the hearse I read "Patrick Massey". Not the dead man, I presume, but the undertaker, whose many-membered family fill a page of the telephone directory with their undertaking establishments and funeral homes. Left past the ranks of priests' graves, rectangular stone boxes like graves of soldiers. Are they standing there, underground, like the Chinese warriors from the emperor's tomb in the exhibition in the Royal Hospital? A cardinal's mausoleum beside an archbishop's, the two dead men in effigy lying stonily in state.

Right turn at the mortuary chapel down the lane of yew trees. It descends gently and the trees make stillness. A funeral party is exiting from the other end. No one belonging to me is buried here. I visit it seldom, the last time for Seán MacBride. One Christ has his right hand raised, another has it down, cupped forward, while his left hand points to his heart. A third Christ has both arms uplifted high like Jim Larkin in O'Connell Street. And now he is crucified on a Celtic cross, or rather, within the circular part of it. Virgins and Little Flowers have their hands joined demurely. Where the cypresses end, on grassless ground a great desolation of old gravestones extends as far as I can see: none with grave-curbs, some fallen, none with flowers. But along the path to the left the graves are curbed and well-kept. Men are mowing grass and cleaning ground. Nearby and at a distance, people are moving with heads down, reading names.

Returning, by another path, in the direction I have come from, I find Dublin Italian graves: Borza, Marsella, Macari. There are small photographs of the dead ones protected by glass. The Italian says, repeatedly, that they were born in Casalattico, died in Dublino. Curious that two graves with Irish names also have the little photographs, as if they had taken example from the adjacent Italians. Husband, wife, husband, wife; wife, husband; husband, wife. Reading from the top down, the husbands have it—they die first. Women do seem to live longer, as one hears, but the dates are often very close, marriages working their lethal chemistry. At the top, level with the chapel, but some distance to the right, there is a row of square slabs, standing slanted for reading. Several of them are covered with dates and names neatly inscribed, the earliest from 1982. I take it they were people who were cremated. The crematorium is a fairly new service. A few steps from the end of the row, and I am looking at Parnell's monument inside a wide circular railing. On a low grassy mound beneath a spreading cypress, a boulder of granite from his native Wicklow with his name on it. Just that, very good.

Across grass I regain the tarmacadamed space, pass the chapel, the O'Connell monument, Roger Casement's grave, and take the first path to the left, the one I last walked down to see Seán MacBride buried. What part of O'Connell is in his tomb? I get confused. His body—he left the *heart* to Rome. A Celtic cross for Sir Charles Gavan Duffy. An erect slab for the First Connaught Rangers Battalion. The Graves of Those Members of the Battalion Who Gave Their Lives during the Mutiny and Subsequently for Irish Freedom. Names, followed respectively by Executed, Shot during Mutiny, Died in Prison, and so on. The next seems to be for hunger-strikers. Not Those Who Can Inflict the Most, But Those Who Can Suffer the Most, Will Conquer. To the left, Thomas Ashe 1917, and others down to Frank Stagg 1977. On the right, Bobby Sands and the nine other Long Kesh men who died after him. Not that their graves are here; it's a memorial. In the centre, in bronze, a torch with figures to either side of it striving upwards. Nurse Eileen O'Farrell, who carried the flag of surrender in 1916, with a verse by Brian O'Higgins. Brian O'Higgins himself. Frank Hugh O'Donnell, John Devoy, Cathal Brugha, James Larkin. Maud Gonne MacBride. Flowers on the earth, still loose from Seán's burial. In behind there the Army party of honour stood, presented arms, and played the Last Post and the Reveille. People were saying the Government had to send them or there would have been a military group of a different hue to render honours. Seán had a past. Through the trees the big greenhouse in the Botanic Gardens. Behind the graves on this side of the path there are two large Republican plots. Around the upper one, among the many names on simple tiles, Countess Markievicz, Peadar Clancy. On the way back, along the path, The O'Rahilly, O'Donovan Rossa, Peadar Kearney who wrote the national anthem, James Stephens, founder of the Fenian Brotherhood. All the great.

In the open space inside the gate three gravediggers, holding shovels, are talking to three photographers. Four more photographers join them. They must be waiting for the Bloom funeral. Clustered near the gate, girls in black leather jackets, short skirts, one with white trousers. Outside, more girls like them, working-class, with young fellows and a woman carrying a baby, pile into a battered blue van and battered old cars. Only one taxi is left, and now before my eyes it's gone. I ask a man what bus would take me to O'Connell Street.

— Any 40, a 40A or B or C, he says.

I stand at the bus stop, watching a continuous procession of big lorries, buses and cars moving into the city. This is the route in from Ashbourne and from Derry on the Foyle. It's seven minutes past twelve. Here comes the Bloom funeral. As I step into the road to see them enter, radiant, laughing, a girl sitting with three other mourners in a car asks me, "What's that, a funeral with an empty hearse?" and I explain to her about Mr Bloom, and she says, looking at the faces of the funeral party, "I've never seen a happy funeral before". A 40A collects me and I go upstairs, sit down and reach for my pipe. But no, it's no smoking. The new rule. They used allow smoking upstairs, that's why I go upstairs. Very radical, the bull by the horns, nowhere set aside for innocent pipe-smokers to delight the travellers with fragrant fumes. Another public amenity gone. I suppose this bus will be travelling by a more normal route. We circle around by Botanic Road to the flowered triangle where I veered off. Happy City, Chinese Meals To Take Away, a Chinese couple passing in front of it. Straight ahead is the straight line to the Liffey that I told my cousin Patricia to take when she came from Omagh.

At Cross Guns Tyres we turn left and, of course, this is it, Whitworth Road, the way the taximan wanted to come. A long line of neat houses straight down to Dorset Street. On our right, in a defile, the railway runs west, the canal above it, the towers of the 'Joy beyond that. Straight ahead there is a clear view down to the docklands. In the bay, apart as ever, the Poolbeg chimneys with their plume of smoke, but in a blue sunlit sky now. Somehow another 40A has got in front, and, as so often happens, two buses of the same number are running together. "Either they don't come or they travel in convoy", as every bus-using Dubliner knows and says. My watch is stopped. A girl tells me it's twenty-five past twelve.

On the bridge as we turn right there is an ad for the Viking Adventure in the crypt of St Audoen's. Viking Dublin reconstructed with live actors. I have gone twice, but not seen it because the queue was too long. O'Mara's Red Parrot pub is another fine Dorset Street specimen. All human life is on this street. Chinese take-away, tobacconist, grocer, butcher, pork butcher, bicycle shop, video club, travel agent, assurance, school of motoring, wallpaper, sign-writer, Indian food, crystal glass, upholstery, and then the same with variants begins all over again. The white Action Hire van appears again, or a brother of it perhaps. Tool Hire, Ladders. So that's what they do. Street-corner signs, Carr-Chaladh/Car Ferries and Dola-Dhroichead/Toll Bridge, point Liffeywards, telling those who don't know.

Hand Gestures in Dublin's Sacred and Secular Statuary. A doctoral thesis. A coffee-table book, with large close-up pictures. Right hand raised, left hand raised, both hands raised—to shoulder level, higher—hands thrust out and down, cupped or flat-palmed hands. Each category with subtle, expressive variations. Add to the world's knowledge. Why not? *Flower Patterns on Ming Plates.*

Down North Frederick Street we return to Parnell Square, but this time past Findlater's Church and the Garden of Remembrance, a quiet place with water which honours those who died for Ireland's freedom. At the Gate, they have Turgenev's *Fathers and Sons*, adapted by Brian Friel. Left now into Parnell Street, stop and out. I cross and turn into O'Connell Street.

Abrakebabra, Seating for 60 Downstairs, offers Doner Kebab £1.95, Shish Kebab ditto, Chicken Kebab £1.85, Mexican Taco ditto, Regular Burger 80p and Tea/Coffee 40p. McGrath's have a Carvery from £2.75, Soup 80p, Quiche, Side Salad and Chips £2.25. In Shades Restaurant Wine Bar, it is Roast Beef, Roast Pork, Gravy, Mint Sauce, all served with Veg. of the Day and Tea or Coffee, £3.25, Dessert extra 60p. Telecom Eireann has nothing for lunch and I cross Cathal Brugha Street to where the Gresham breathes cool elegance over the wide pavement. Awnings, window-boxes and canopy in dark blue against the white stone. Antóin Mac Fhionghaile, a man of my name, owns the parked empty bus from distant Glenties. I'd put the private bus-owners in charge of running the country. High in the southern sky, beyond O'Connell Bridge, the sun, blazing unhampered, pours its light with abandon down the full length of the street. The Savoy, in one of its five in-house cinemas, is showing *Three Men and a Baby*. At the Carlton, beyond the roadworks, *Fatal Attraction* is still running. My raincoat, reflected in the big windows of Pizzaland, looks absurd. Two French girls with rucksacks have emerged from Tourist Information and are heading for Burger King on the corner of Cathedral Street. The name exaggerates, for the church down that street, hidden away, is the Catholic Pro-Cathedral. Dublin has no Catholic cathedral but two Protestant ones, to confuse Yves Person and other tourists. Beshoff's, Three Generations of Quality. They first gave us fish and chips with glamour and style on Westmoreland Street, and later here, though I have not been in it. Whiting £1.17, Mackerel the same, Lemon Sole £1.38, Haddock £1.63, Ray £1.97. What with shops selling tripper trash, and fast-food and gambling parlours, and huckster garishness of all kinds, O'Connell Street had gone to the dogs, and is still not

50

back from them. But a clean-up has been taking place; the worst shop signs are gone, fronts are improving. This stretch from Cathedral Street to the Café Kylemore at North Earl Street has taken the lead. The gold-lettered names on black for Shasha's and Beshoff's, and on dark green for the Kylemore, set the tone. Beshoff's large windows are set in black wood. The Kylemore's, slightly darkened and bearing delicate plant tracings, are surrounded by dark brown wood. You enter by revolving doors and sit at marble tables. It reflects nostalgia for a certain seemlinesss after the slapdash, all-in-shirtsleeves style that set in with the 60s. "As the new-rich masses reached out to seize hold of the good life, it lowered its standards to greet them. How were they to know?" Lasagna with Garlic Bread is £2.70, Two Jumbo Sausages and Chips £2.60. For the Lunch Special £1.99, see blackboard inside. Downes's cakeshop used to stand here. In a verse put in the mouth of Joyce's outraged Dublin publisher, it found a place in literature.

> Shite and onions! Do you think I'll print
> The name of the Wellington Monument,
> Sydney parade and Sandymount tram,
> Downes's cakeshop and Williams's jam.

From McDowell's The Happy Ring House I cross to the fence around Anna Livia and, finding a gap, step inside. She is a green, very slender, austere lady, seated and leaning back, merging with the water which flows down over her and bubbles around her long legs.

12.40 - 1.20

O'CONNELL STREET VIA THE *INDEPENDENT* OFFICE TO ABBEY STREET

On the paved empty Pillar space, flowers are selling, and a young man has done the Mona Lisa in chalk, with a Sacred Heart, just the heart, beneath it. A double-decker, painted all over for Philishave the Electric Shaver, stands at the lights. In the Pillar's days this was the terminus for many trams and buses; now, the trams gone, the buses end their journeys in many places, but not here. Crowds flow the full breadth of pedestrianised Henry Street, the leading shopping boulevard of the Northside. Under the columns of Francis Johnston's great and everlasting GPO they're selling T-shirts for the European Soccer Finals. "Fun Run Carnage"— I have seen those words already—on the *Irish News* from Belfast. "Could Have Maimed Hundreds" says the *Evening Press*, and you know that it's about the bomb in Lisburn. The crowds surge on, glad it's not here. Jim Larkin, his back turned, has his hands upraised as I remembered him in Glasnevin, except that there is a suggestion, in the spread of the fingers perhaps, of a shaman conjuring dead souls into life.

I turn into Prince's Street and am depressed by the drear aspect of the British Home Stores which replaced, in the 70s, the splendid Metropole—cinema, restaurant and dance-hall. A bicycle park on the footpath extends the full length of its windows. A van is leaving the *Independent's* back entrance. They are loaded there with newspapers. Reaching it, I pass between two vans to a glass cubicle where a man sits, and tell him that Bruce Arnold is expecting me. He says to go through a door, continue along a corridor, and make my way to the leader-writers' office on the first floor.

Through the corridor, and through rooms where journalists sit at word-processors—Bruce is going to show me the new technology—I reach and mount the main stairs towards the front of the building and find him in the leader-writers' office. He is being interviewed and tape-recorded by a young man with a North American accent who is asking him what he thinks of Yeats as poet, politician and man. The door squeaked as I opened it and squeaks again as I close it. Bruce turns his head momentarily while beginning to answer the question, and I say:

—I'm sorry I'm late, but I see you're not worried.

—a wonderful lyric poet, an interesting, but arrogant and elitist man, Bruce is saying to the interviewer. As a politician, I think he had an old-fashioned view of the world, to put it no more strongly than that.

—Do you think, asks the interviewer, that was part of the whole romanticism that affected his nature?

—I believe Yeats as a thinker lacked any centre. He inherited a curious Irish phenomenon which was a dependence on a confusion out of which some sense might, or might not, emerge by the exercise of poetry on it. So he seizes on images and ideas out of a wide variety of sources—the tattered ragged man, figures out of Irish mythology, figures derived from the English poetic tradition, the William Blake kind of world, and puts them into enormously moving, wonderfully lyrical poems which quite often don't make sense. I think that one of the offshoots of that was that Yeats was never able to mount a sustained, substantial long poem. Given his long life and large output, and the great amount of material he apparently

53

absorbed, he should have created at least one great twentieth-century epic poem. But it was beyond his capacity because he didn't think that way. An Irish poet whom I knew well and whom I admired, a man out of fashion and out of his time, called Monk Gibbon, began a poem about Yeats with the line "That wrong-headed old man whose phrase was always right". And I always think that about Yeats. I think he was wrong-headed. He was wrong-headed in the specific political attitudes he took in the 30s. He was wrong-headed, in the more fundamental way for a poet, of adapting and taking over for himself ideas and concepts—some of the theosophical material that was churning around at the beginning of the century, for example—and rendering it meaningless in his poetry—though he did this beautifully.

I stand up and open the door to go out until Bruce is ready. Both men turn their heads.

—Don't mind me, I say, I wasn't listening, but it sounded delightful.

—No, no, say both of them together, please, please!

—I've introduced you in advance of your arrival, says Bruce. This is Colin Henderson of the Canadian Broadcasting Corporation. Just sit tight.

I close the door and sit down again.

—So you take exception, says Henderson, to the view that Yeats hammered together a great unity, a symbolic universe, that one critic has described as more solid than that of any poet since Wordsworth.

—That's completely wrong. I would take issue with that absolutely and totally. I don't think it's there. I think it's a sham and a charade. It's terribly unfashionable these days to level criticisms of this kind against Yeats. But his background material simply doesn't hold together. There isn't a unity there. As Literary Editor, I see a vast number of books on Yeats. I see the raw material of the Yeats industry. It comes across my desk week in, week out. A lot of it I set aside, some of it I send out for review. But much of it is really quite pretentious nonsense, and in some instances I've been able to prove this by going back to members of the family, and simply asking them is this the right explanation. Last year I had a most interesting conversation with Michael Yeats in Monte Carlo. Some lines of a poem had come up and Michael was giving me the real source of them—I forget the details, but it had something to do with the chickens they kept in their back garden in Dundrum and the next-door dog which had chased and killed one of them. It was a lovely anecdote which Michael Yeats told me with much laughter and fun. And then he pointed to something by an American scholar who had given amazing, high-flown sources for the lines, which simply were not true. There was no way they could be true.

There is silence for a moment and then Henderson says:

—Yeats on his deathbed. Seamus Heaney described Yeats on his deathbed as like Macbeth on the battlements looking out over the woods of Birnam and seeing them move.

—I heard him saying that yesterday, says Bruce, at a session of the literary conference out in Dún Laoghaire, and I was fascinated because I admire Heaney a great deal. But I think he is one of the most astute and clever managers of his own position as a poet, and of his own career, to the point where, though I am sure he has doubts and reservations about great areas of Yeats's life and work, he would be the last person to express those other than in that sort of elliptical language. It's the sort of language where you pause and wonder 'What does he mean?' Does he mean that Yeats at the end of his life saw the distortion and wobbliness of much of the theory which lay behind his own poetry? Or what does he mean? It is critical, and yet obscure enough not to quite fit in with the awful trauma which that sight must have represented for Macbeth.

—M-hm, says Henderson. I interpreted it in a number of ways, but I thought that part of it conveyed Yeats's recognition that much of what he had believed in his life was simply not true.

—I would go further than that, says Bruce. I think that Yeats hadn't ever fully believed in it, certainly not in a coherent way. The writer, the artist generally, is engaged in a permanent hunt for meaning and belief. You are looking for things to believe in, ideas and concepts and things. Even in a poet as integrated as T.S. Eliot—who in my judgment in the twentieth century is the absolute antithesis of W.B. Yeats — nevertheless there is this reaching out, these vast grasps for Eastern literature or religious points or African tribal rituals. "Haruspicate and scry", he said. You look at the entrails, trying to divine what's going to happen in the future. All of this is grist to the poetic mill. But in the case of Yeats I think this search led to a lot of confusion, and I genuinely think that's an Irish attribute. I think this confusion is a Celtic thing, that there is a principle of confusion in the Celtic mind, part of which Yeats inherited. Of course he also inherited a quite different thing. He once said that all his roots as a poet lay in the *English* poetic tradition, went back to Blake. Now when that was said in Monte Carlo last year, it created enormous division and friction and almost verbal violence between people like Denis Donoghue and American critics who were quite urbane about it. But the Irish people there didn't want to let slip the Irish antecedents for Yeats.

—Late in his life he invented an ancestry for himself among the Ascendancy, didn't he? He claimed Burke and Berkeley, Swift and Goldsmith.

—I think every Protestant Anglo-Irish person would do that in the same circumstances. One of my perspectives on Yeats, again an unfashionable and indeed an unpopular one, is that I approach him through artists and writers like Orpen and George Moore, with whom I have great affinities. They couldn't stand the literary revival. Moore simply went, and

Orpen did the same. They were successful in their different arts, painting and writing, on an international scale, and they thought the atmosphere in Dublin had a kind of hothouse intensity, with everyone either patting each other on the back or being pushed out of the fold and excluded from the literary whirlpool. They had an amused view of Yeats; they poked fun at him. Orpen made funny drawings of him, accentuating his willowy, tall, master-poet appearance. He guyed the whole thing, and Moore in his own way did the same.

—Do you have a funny story about Yeats, a favourite anecdote that shows a side of his character?

—Not really. I love the images that Monk Gibbon produced of him. When Gibbon as a young poet went to see him, Yeats would strike an attitude. He would be leaning out the window on Merrion Square, looking out over the traffic. He would know that this young nervous poet was behind him, and he would deliberately go on staring out at the evening light, or something like that, in order to create a theatrical relationship between them. And then he'd turn and say, "Ah, Monk Gibbon, you're very welcome". A putting-down relationship really. Something of that was reflected later in the *Oxford Book of Modern Verse*, where Yeats left out notable poets, and put in safe people who were admirers of his. He kept out, for example, Austin Clarke, who by 1937 or thereabouts, when the book was published, had a considerable and I think very deserved reputation as a different kind of Irish poet. And he was a man who would have benefited enormously from inclusion by Yeats. I think there was a jealousy there.

—Wasn't it Clarke who said that writing after Yeats was like being in the shadow of a great tree?

—Well, I think they all felt that. I don't think it was necessarily adulation that motivated that statement. Yeats *was* a great tree. The shadow he cast was absolutely huge. It was rather like for the prose writers the impact of Joyce. You

don't necessarily admire Joyce to recognise that you are
writing prose under the shadow of Joyce's enormous impact on
twentieth-century fiction. In many respects I think Joyce has
had a devastating effect—more because of how he has been
taken up by generation after generation of students. Yeats is in
the same category. Mercifully, a lovely Irish poet like Paddy
Kavanagh seems so far to have escaped this attention. People
in Dublin can still read him without this enormous weight of
shadow that hangs over Yeats and Joyce, distorting our ability
to see the wood for the trees—and distorting our willingness
to point out the weaknesses in W.B. Yeats which I think are
very considerable. In the final analysis, I accept the father's
comment that he would be remembered as the father of the
painter, of the brother, and I put forward the unfashionable
idea that there was more cohesion and integrity in Jack Yeats
than there is in W. B. It so happens that monuments are
built by money, by fashion, and by vested interests which
become impregnable. Take the monument to the Impres-
sionist painters: they're effectively indestructible, as a great
corpus of valuable art at the end of the nineteenth century.
Nobody's prepared to say boo to any of them, though some of
them are very poor painters. Much the same is true of Yeats.

—There are graduate schools across North America which
would simply collapse under the weight of that criticism if it
were ever accepted.

—I know, that's right. It's monstrous really. Desmond, you
have a different view, I'm sure.

Henderson turns to me and says:

—Is that true? What do you think of Yeats?

—I suppose, I say, Bruce said that because I'm a Catholic
Irishman and someone he'd regard as a nationalist or republican. I've a different background from Bruce, who is English
in fact—right, Bruce? You're not Anglo-Irish, are you?

—No, I'm English.

—When I heard you talking there about the Anglo-Irish,

I was beginning to wonder had you antecedents among them. Anyhow I'm one of the natives, with a fairly typical background. You know, first generation to university in my family, ever, that sort of thing. Came up with the Revolution and the Free State to the light of day.

—You're the class that Yeats feared, aren't you? says Henderson.

—I'm that class, yes. But of course, so was Joyce for that matter, only before me. On my mother's side my grandfather came from the Sperrin Mountains in County Tyrone, and was an Irish-speaker in his youth—among the few Irish-speakers then left in what is called Northern Ireland today. He came to Belfast and spent his life there as a second-class citizen when things were at their worst under Stormont. My mother and her brothers grew up there. I was born in Belfast, my father was a Sligoman. And as I said, neither on his side nor hers had anybody in the family ever been to university. We weren't, in other words, even of that more successful Catholic background of which there was a minority in Yeats's time—the Catholic bourgeoisie, or that section of them who were called Castle Catholics. Like most of my contemporaries at college in Dublin, I was entering the world for the first time, getting hold of modern knowledge and techniques, languages—which I was good at.

—How did this emerging Catholic middle class view Yeats?

—My people came to Dublin, and I grew up as a middle-class Dubliner, went to Belvedere, where Joyce had been, and then on to UCD, my parents pushing all the time for me to break into what they had been excluded from—what people like them had been excluded from because they didn't have the education. How did Yeats and Douglas Hyde and the rest seem to us? I say Douglas Hyde, whom I admire more profoundly, certainly as a mind, than Yeats. He is a neglected major intellect of the Irish twentieth century. His insight was enormous into the process of the Revolution and so on, and how language and culture could be motivating forces for other things. But anyway, those people, and Lady Gregory and the rest, were in my eyes rootless colonists who sought roots in the kind of thing that my people were abandoning—abandoning, don't forget, by their own volition, rapidly. Those who still could speak Irish in the nineteenth century were beating their children, and having their teachers beat them, if they spoke Irish. Going for English, wanting to get hold of the English culture to get on in life—while Yeats and Gregory and Douglas Hyde, these rootless colonists, were turning back to that thing which the Catholic middle class, and would-be Catholic middle class, were abandoning.

—So this was part of the reason that people say Yeats never saw Ireland realistically?

—Well, of course, he *saw* that Ireland that I'm talking about—and satirised it—as "fumbling in the greasy till".

—Biddy and Paudeen. . .

—Yes, that's the Catholic middle class. That's the people, precisely, who had no more regard for the Ireland he valued—ancient Ireland, Gaelic Ireland, western peasant Ireland—than the majority of his co-religionists. For, of course, Yeats was a renegade Protestant. That's a point I'd make in relation to what Bruce was saying about practically any Irish Protestant being likely to look back towards Berkeley and Burke and so on as their ancestors. A lot of them were too philistine, and still today are too philistine, to be interested in that sort of ancestry. Yeats certainly was a renegade and so were Douglas Hyde and Lady Gregory. They were rebelling against the ordinary middle-class Protestant culture of their time. And of course in all of this we're talking about Protestants outside the northeast, where it's all very special, and where they would definitely not regard Berkeley, Burke or any of those people as having anything to do with them. They feel closer to the Scottish Protestant tradition, the Presbyterians there certainly, but many of the others too. But the point I was making was that Yeats was out of sympathy with Protestant as well as Catholic middle-class culture. He was anti-middle class. He was a would-be aristocrat. He was doing the kind of thing that middle-class individuals had done all over Europe for a hundred years, except that the normal way for them to be anti-bourgeois was to adhere to the working class, to socialism. Most of the leading socialists were middle-class persons.

— Is there a backlash now, given that Irish Studies are seen as so essential to Irish nationalism? It seems to me that there is much more regard for Irish mythology, for a forgotten past, in Ireland today.

— Well, there is and there isn't. It depends on what Ireland you are moving in. In this city of Dublin there is a large section of the population who don't give a damn about Irish mythology or any other mythology, and think that myth is a silly or an evil thing. They are the very opposite of having regard for myth of any kind—they pride themselves on being practical, realistic, tough people. I'm talking very much of young people too. They're materialists. That's a large part of Irish life today, much as in other parts of the western world. But as it happens there's an important influence from outside Ireland nourishing our interest in our mythical past. And that's the vogue for the Celts in Europe today, which links up with the vogue for the Red Indian culture in North America. The whole alternative culture, the New Age kind of philosophy—the Celts are really big in that. I'm getting endless literature these past months from Hallein in Austria where some of the oldest Celtic traces are to be found, and they are advertising their *Keltensommer*, a whole programme of Celtic entertainments, Celtic studies and so on.

— The idea that there's a forgotten wisdom.

— Yes, the druids, of whom we know practically nothing apart from a few stray remarks in Latin and Greek authors.

61

For that very reason a lot has been attributed to them. The druids are supposed to have had that wisdom which the modern world lacks. But anyhow here in Dublin bookshops you see books by British authors on the Celts, books translated from French or German. The Celts, as I said, are a big thing at the moment. So obviously that links up in Irish consciousness, or rather, among a number of educated Irish people, with what comes out of our own tradition. And so a certain interest in all of that is kept alive.

—To come back to Yeats, says Henderson. Would you summarise his achievement?

—I think that the side of him that was a visionary explainer of the world, the philosophical side, has been excessively neglected in our view of him in Ireland, and in our approach to him here—because we don't like philosophy in this country. I happen to like philosophy, you see. But it is an unusual activity in Ireland in the past few centuries, to try to explain the world, and to have an independent vision of the world. And Yeats did work out such a vision, quite apart from his poetry. That is one side of him, and you can't bring it directly together with his contemporary political poetry, or his love poetry, which is another voice speaking, another persona. Then again, there is a real gap between the poet of the early, what you might call pre-Raphaelite poems, and the poetry of the 1920s and 30s. So what is there definitive you can say about Yeats? He wasn't Anglo-Ireland come into its voice. He transcended such categories. He was also Ireland. I very much regard him, whatever they were saying in Monte Carlo, as an Irish poet. He may have his roots in the English poetic tradition, but then can't one say that, apart from the influence from Patrick Kavanagh, Heaney has too? The extent to which Heaney, starting out, rode along with what was going on in English poetry, was considerable. And in a sense, indeed, he has continued to be more a part of English poetry than of the Irish poetry tradition in English that Yeats and others founded.

—I always understood there to be a big change in the form of Yeats's romanticism from the early poetry which was a longing for escape, for a vision of beauty, pre-Raphaelite women—

—And for very unserious fairies, I interject. He was later to discover that fairies are very serious.

—Yes, continues Henderson, there was that part of him. And then there was a disillusionment at the turn of the century, disappointment that he had not got a popular audience, that people weren't in tune with him, and that Maud Gonne went off and got married, and he started to read Nietzsche. So there was this big change in him, and his romanticism became a kind of defiant heroism or tragic joy. He decided he must "fight against the ungovernable sea". And that was his posture in the last part of his life, with Cúchulainn as his *alter ego*.

—As you talked, what occurred to me was that perhaps the most wonderful thing about Yeats was that he kept facing up to everything, to all his difficulties, in poetry, and this great, sculpted voice came out which for me has the sonorousness of those great Roman inscriptions where the lettering is so beautiful. Complete and rounded and firm. He managed that kind of poetry. It comes through to me like nothing else written in the twentieth century. It has the power of Shakespeare, that power of verse to sweep you away. And he managed to handle everything from the private to the politically public in that verse, and to adorn it, and to make out of it a sort of *aes aeternum*—a thing forever sculpt in bronze. Through all those vicissitudes you talk about, all those disappointments, he spoke it all in great verse.

Henderson turns back to Bruce and says:

—Respond.

—I would disagree, says Bruce, in this sense. All the things that Desmond has just said, really they apply infinitely more closely, and in a more integrated fashion, to

T.S. Eliot than they do to Yeats. Eliot saw the great contrast in twentieth-century poetry as being between himself and Yeats. They were totally different. If you want somebody who charts the twentieth century right the way through—obviously he lived through much more of it—Eliot in my opinion hits the nail on the head again and again, whereas Yeats goes off at tangents and goes up blind alleys about psychic forces, fascism, political balance, whereas Eliot in *The Waste Land*, "Ash Wednesday", the *Four Quartets*, repeatedly brings himself back to the very centre, the heart, of what the modern world is at. And if you regard as perhaps the blackest passage of the twentieth century that associated with Naziism, and the isolation of Britain, and the difficulties during the early 40s for the Allied powers—the huge threat of European fascism against the world—it's Eliot whose finger is on the pulse in those four poems. Yeats, up until his death, was wide of the reality. He was dealing with something that didn't really apply to the lives that all of us are now leading. Yeats of course provides material for research—much more so than Eliot. He has all those wonderful avenues down which people scurry with their notebooks and tape-recorders finding out what people who knew Yeats believed him to mean. There isn't anything like that industry surrounding Eliot, because Eliot's language is the language of real people through the 20s, 30s and 40s.

—I would actually agree, I say, that Eliot deals more squarely and profoundly with the twentieth-century experience than Yeats does. However, that isn't what I was saying. What I was saying was that Yeats, faced with the various encounters and vicissitudes of *his* life, of his path through life, squared up to each of those in verse and produced great verse in response to them. He didn't take the twentieth century, globally, as his theme to the extent that Eliot did.

The tape clicks to an end and Colin Henderson says:
—Well, that's it.

—Have you been filling tapes around the town? I ask him.

—I did some yesterday at the literary conference, he says.

I had arranged with Bruce to accompany me to Davy Byrne's for lunch, but now he says:

—I'm sorry, Desmond, I'm afraid I can't come to lunch. A crisis has blown up with the Editor about the books page and I have to go and see him.

—I'd like to come along, says Henderson, if that's all right.

I tell him that's fine, and that I'll meet him in five minutes on Abbey Street at the side-door to Eason's.

I leave by the Abbey Street exit, where the *Irish Catholic* used to be, turn left and walk as far as Eason's side-door, cross the street and continue through Bachelor's Way, past side and back entrances and J.L. Smallman Plumbers Merchants, to the quay called Bachelor's Walk. From above Royal Liver Assurance on the far quay the sun shines in my eyes. To the left, O'Connell Bridge, the city's nodal point, with its line of chubby, graceful balusters. That's enough about Yeats and Joyce for one day. There are people in this country, literary intellectuals, who cannot open their mouths about anything to do with Ireland today without saying, "as Yeats put it so well, quote", or "what Joyce called, quote", and that's supposed to be an end of the matter. I am in a quandary about my raincoat. It is light, but it is still absurd to be wearing it in this sun. But its pockets are useful for my pipe things and camera, and I need a hand free to carry my plastic bag with maps and miscellaneous, and another hand free for my tape-recorder. Pondering this, I decide on balance that it is easier and more convenient to wear it and sweat.

I turn right past furniture showrooms and Harding's bicycle shop and the Irish Church Missions—Obtain Salvation through the Lord Jesus Christ—and stop at the Pierrot Snooker Club with its antiquated front and large plants standing in the windows, Open 24 Hours, New Video Games, Snack Bar, Seven Days a Week. I cross through the traffic to the quay wall. Across the river, a line of buses, dark and light green, stands along Aston Quay outside what used to be McBirney's famous store, and is now, I read, Virgin Megastore. A year, two years, three months, you omit to stop and look at a stretch of familiar street in central Dublin, and then, when you do look, it is not familiar any more. But the arc of the Metal Bridge endures, and people are moving across it continuously as in that Arabian fable of the bridge as an image of life and death; the bridge in which trapdoors open randomly, swallowing now him, now her. The Metal Bridge, or as some call it, the Ha'penny Bridge, has found new life since the Temple Bar area on the south bank came alive these last years, and a shoppers' track was beaten through it from South Great George's Street to Liffey Street on the north bank, Mary Street and Henry Street beyond; and vice versa. The sunlight shimmers on the empty river, but its most splendid illumination is on the south bank far to the left, on that tall, white fairy-castle building standing where D'Olier and Westmoreland Streets converge towards O'Connell Bridge. Tall, that is, by pre-60s standards, for in fact its loftiness is outdone physically, though not spiritually, by the off-white office-block that opposes it across D'Olier Street and points a tall radio mast at the sky. High on its face a clock says l.15, and beneath the clock, vertically, like neon signs in Japanese cities: SONY Radio TV Radio Hi Fi.

I return to Bachelor's Way, and passing through it glimpse "Peace Love Anarchy" on a wall. Henderson is waiting for me at Eason's side-door.

1.20 - 3.05

ABBEY STREET VIA DAVY BYRNE'S
TO KILDARE STREET

I have heard that some Joycean group, yesterday or the day before, inserted bronze plaques in the pavement from here to Davy Byrne's to mark Leopold Bloom's itinerary. So I look for the plaque, and see it and show it to Henderson. It depicts Leopold walking, a Georgian doorway in the background. Beside that, the words "AEOLUS The office of THE EVENING TELEGRAPH. Chapter 7", and underneath the lot, "Proudly sponsored by Cantwell and Cochrane (Dublin) Ltd". We cross the street at the Dublin Millennium Office—or one of them rather, there's another in the Royal Hibernian Way—and through glass see people eating Kentucky Fried Chicken at tables for two.

—What part of Canada are you from? I ask Henderson.

—Halifax, Nova Scotia, he says or at least that's where I'm living now.

At the corner with O'Connell Street we turn right, and there is William Smith O'Brien on his pedestal. For a hesitant rebellion in a cabbage-patch he won his place among the immortals. After a few paces I stop at the Super X Drugstore.

—This used to be Lemon's sweet shop.

It is in supermarket style, with hairsprays, shampoos and small cosmetic sets on the shelves, and there is a machine for weighing yourself, and packets of Smarties sweets.

A plaque like the first one is set in the footpath, but this time with the words "Pineapple rock, lemon platt, butter scotch . . . among the warm sweet fumes of Graham Lemon's. p.124". We continue past a Playland gaming parlour, an Apollo discount shop and cheap restaurants. That man calling "Flowers a pound a bunch" held a bunch in front of him with a very rigid, outstretched arm, his face serious, alienated from his action, as if disowning both it and the flowers. Opposite O'Connell's Late Night Pharmacy the great man stands among his guardian angels cloaked, his back to us. Hundreds of people are surging along the wide footpath, some carrying plastic bags, many of them office-workers in their lunch-break, engaged in errands or heading for food. Many girls are in colourful summer dresses, but they are not wearing as much white as other days, probably because today started dull. Nearly half of the men are jacketless. At the curb of Bachelor's Walk a little green man in the traffic-light opposite indicates that we can cross onto O'Connell Bridge, as wide as it is long.

Millennium flags flutter at its four corners. Their central coloured design, on a white background, seems to be a stylised version of the city's coat of arms. I suppose that, since Nelson's Pillar was blown up, this is as near as you could pinpoint "the centre of the city". Downriver, above the statue of Lady Commerce on the Custom House dome, the tall green crane that stood motionless earlier is moving in a lofty arc. I glance at the long traffic-island running along the middle of the bridge, half-expecting to see someone with a poster pleading a cause or making a protest; but there is no one.

—People stand there sometimes, I tell Henderson, with a poster or slogan, making a point.

I remember—I could not forget—how in the long days of the H-Block hunger-strike up to a dozen walked there daily amid the traffic flow, displaying large posters, first with the

68

face of Bobby Sands, then with the faces of the other fasting or dying men, one of them maybe known to be about to die, or just dead. The traffic slowed or stopped or turned past them as they tramped out an ellipse day after day, boring into our consciousness. Today the only permanent human occupants of the bridge are the trinket-sellers along the balustrade, two girls and three young men. Their wares are displayed mostly on vertical boards covered with black velvet, but also, horizontally, in barrows. You can have your name on a silver-plated chain for £2, Deirdre, Emma, Eileen, or you can buy earrings large or small, pewter, leather or seashell, and leather bangles or purses, and chokers, necklaces, torques or brooches, brass or copper, and badges that say Volkswagen, Texas Rangers or Marshal, Dobb City, or that are shaped like stars or guns or planes or men, or that say I—then a picture of a heart—Kerry, Cork or Dublin, or Ireland in its Tricolour colours; and at 30p, or two for 50p, badges that say *Póg mo Thóin*, I Hate School, Say No to Drugs, Help the Gardaí—Beat Yourself Up, and tapes of The New Order, Bob Dylan, The Beatles or The Waterboys, and decorative patches at £1, or large ones for £2.95, of James Dean or Bomber Squadron US Navy. At the Aston Quay kerb, a little red man in the light tells us not to cross, but the people cross nevertheless, playing games with the traffic, and we move forward with them but get stopped for a time in the middle by an onset of vehicles turning left from Westmoreland Street.

Beginning at the corner where the Ballast Office stood, and where Abrakebabra now sells fast, magic food, an iron railing runs along the right-hand kerb for about 60 yards, and another of equal length opposite it; so we cannot cross Westmoreland Street where I would like to. Instead, grasping the lie of things, we cross to a large island, back in the direction of the bridge; a veritable desert island, which might stand, with that name, as a "sculpture" in a Rosc exhibition.

On its expanse of stone flag lapped by street, its five inani-
mate inhabitants—a tall slender grey lamp-post, a battery of
traffic lights attached parasitically to it, two more such
batteries standing on their own posts, a circular No Right
Turn sign similarly hoisted, and a yellow and blue light-
bollard four feet tall—relate to each other, desolately, forming a group but no community, like characters in a Beckett
play. Up Westmoreland Street, at its far end, the pillared
portico of the Bank of Ireland juts out at an angle towards
Trinity College. It juts out more than I remember it doing,
but almost certainly it cannot move and—though they are
always changing the city—it has hardly been moved. Weathered fixtures of the Dublin landscape, the Bank and the
College, Scylla and Charybdis, looking towards each other
now much as they did in the eighteenth century when the
Bank was the Parliament.

—I was reading recently, I say aloud, an old account of
this part of Dublin as it was in 1757, when the Rotunda
Hospital was built. The city-centre then was upriver and
Trinity College a suburban campus. On this side of it, there
was a collection, I quote, of "wretched sheds and thatched
cabins", and from them you walked to the sandy river bank
here through two narrow lanes. You passed barbers' shops,
lime-kilns and saw-pits. And then you got on a ferry-boat
here which took you across the river to another dirty strand
where you made your way through a couple of lanes to about
where the GPO is now. That's where the Mall, the only part
of O'Connell Street that was built then, began. Hard to
imagine, isn't it?

—Sure is, says Henderson.

Leaving the island, when the lights allow, we cross to the
other footpath of Westmoreland Street, where it makes a
V-turn into D'Olier Street, beside the fairy-castle building
that looked so white in the sunlight from Bachelor's Walk
and now appears cream-coloured. Purcell's, tobacconist and

sweet-shop—a tobacconist's of the old kind with jars to make mixtures, and experts in charge—used occupy the ground floor, making this corner bright and animated. Now the building or most of it stands empty, and I can see decorators' accoutrements through the window. In the stone over its side-door on Westmoreland Street, where a sign says Lafayette, Photographer, an inscription with coats of arms conveys that the London and Lancashire Fire Insurance Company were the original owners. There is a hairdresser's down a stairs in the basement.

—I'll ask there, I'm curious, I say to Henderson.

In the hairdresser's a girl turns aside from cutting a man's hair and says that it belongs to the ICS Building Society next door. Pondering on the significance of that, I return and exclaim:

—The dead spreading hand of finance. You see the ICS there, with their big building. You'd think that would be enough for them, but they own this too.

And then we observe, as we proceed up the left-hand side of Westmoreland Street towards Fleet Street which intersects it, that the ICS is followed by Irish Life Building Society, and then, after two empty buildings and the Dublin Pharmacy— where you can get cheap frames for your glasses and where I got my last frame after I had broken it by having it in my hip-pocket and bending down—the long stretch of the Educational Building Society to the Fleet Street corner.

—You know, I say to Henderson, I remember when this side of the street was alive—look how few people are walking on it now compared to the other side. There was a fish-shop and the Paradiso coffee-shop with a late-night place in the roof, and two men's outfitters, and the *Irish Times* with its clock, and, a long time ago, when I was a student, the Gaelic magazine *Comhar* used have its office upstairs in that last stretch beyond Fleet Street. You see now those— how many?—five houses there. They belong to

Allied Irish Banks and three of them are standing empty, and look there, in Fleet Street, adjoining them, the Pearl Bar, it's dead too. It used to be a great *Irish Times* place.

—I recognise the pattern, says Henderson. It's the same everywhere.

But as we reach the College Street corner, opposite the Bank of Ireland, I realise that that is not the end of the story. It seems as if the financial quarter, off to the right up there in Dame Street past the Bank, is stretching out to seize Westmoreland Street and reach O'Connell Bridge. Even on the far side where, towards the bridge, Bewley's coffee-house, a discount shop, Beshoff's palatial chip shop and others, still hold out and draw crowds along that footpath, finance has its outrunners: Bank of Ireland Chambers housing Brennan Insurances, and another EBS office and the Agricultural Credit Corporation. A queue stands at the money-dispensing machine near the side-door of the Bank of Ireland, and I notice, first, that the Mormons who used recruit there, and the pavement artists, are gone; second, that there are two severe little black notices on the deserted railing—the Bank, doubtless, asserting its right to its frontage, and to have its money-collecting customers undisturbed. I was surprised to read recently that the Bank of Ireland bought the old Parliament building as far back as 1802, only two years after the Union. One of the conditions was that the Bank must alter its exterior in such a way as to "reconcile the citizens" to the change of function; another, that both Chambers of Parliament should be completely altered. But the Bank did not implement this in the House of Lords, where concerts are sometimes held today, and which people tell me is splendid. We cross to the island in College Street which Thomas Moore shares with a public lavatory and four telephone boxes, and then to the footpath that brings us around the front of Trinity College, Edmund Burke behind the railing, Dame Street to the right, and traffic curving off into it past Grattan and Eddie Delaney's statue of Thomas Davis in a greatcoat. At the entrance to Trinity, people, as always, are waiting for people, and beyond it, from behind the railing, Goldsmith watches them.

I always have to remind myself that Grafton Street begins here between Oliver Goldsmith and James Fox and Co.'s old tobacco shop. It is not what people *mean* by Grafton Street, which begins a hundred yards further up, where Nassau Street turns off to the left taking the Trinity railing with it, and Suffolk Street opens on the right hand. The gate of the Provost's House is open and there are flower-boxes on the window-sills. And then we cross Nassau Street into Grafton Street proper, marked by its new-laid reddish bricks for walking softly, and kerbless since all of it is footpath. The fragrances of the Body Shop, bubbles for my lady love. Apart from Holland's perhaps, on William Street in Galway, I have never seen customers constantly thronging a newsagent's as they do the Bus Stop, so that squads of assistants are kept busy constantly. Perhaps it is because it has no front wall or door, but stands wide open; and many of the customers, of course, are buying sweets. Down narrow Adam's Court to the left, Jammet's back-bar used to be; which was as near as I ever got to that famous, expensive restaurant. A great place to be in those late afternoons which, in the manner of Dublin, could lead to adventures reaching deep into the night. A great place for oysters. I had assumed it closed when the restaurant closed twenty years ago, but then, a month ago, I heard someone talk of a Mac's Bar there. The name has stayed with me because I never heard it given to any bar but *Maic's*, *Tigh Mhaic*, in Cárna, Conamara, which I drank in for eleven years.

—Just a second, I say, and I run down the lane.

But there is no bar, only backs and sides and dead walls and windows. We walk on past McDonalds of the hamburgers and between the many windows of Brown Thomas and Switzer's, gazed at by dummies wearing beautiful clothes, a sight now entangled in my mind with the people picking clothes off the tarmacadam at the Saturday market in Cumberland Street.

—I like this street, says Henderson, it definitely has an air to it.

A girl who has just been given a present by another girl opens it, finds it's marzipan, laughs and says, "Thanks, Liz". A girl in jeans in the middle of the street is playing a violin. Brown Thomas has extended its fenestral empire to Duke Street and around its corner, displacing Combridge's old art gallery whose name-sign still shows. At the corner, or rather on both corners, the flower-women are displaying stacked tulips, irises, daffodils, freesia, statis, carnations and roses, the seasons rendered irrelevant by the wonders of modern international transport.

In Duke Street as we turn into it, ahead of us on the right, a small crowd clusters outside Davy Byrne's, and some of them are holding glasses of Guinness or red wine. Held by the sight, we see a girl at the door selling single red carnations and yellow roses. Thinking fast I say to Henderson "Blooms", and he says "I get it". We reach the pub and glance inside and it appears that those outside are not so much sun-lovers as an overflow: inside the drinkers are standing packed. Neither at the door nor inside are they the usual Davy Byrne's clientele of auctioneers, bankers, stockbrokers and lawyers, accountants and people from Switzer's and Brown Thomas, or they are that only in small part and submerged. Henderson shakes his head, saying "Too crowded for me, I'll try the Bailey", and I say, "Maybe I'll see you later". He leaves to cross to the storied Bailey, where Parnell and his friends used gather, where Trinity students and general drop-outs usually throng, and where the original door of No. 7 Eccles Street is preserved thanks to John Ryan, once landlord of the premises, bar and restaurant. Patrick Kavanagh, when he stalked through Dublin, unveiled it with the words: "I hereby declare this door shut".

In Davy Byrne's, forcing a passage with my shoulders and hips parallel on my left to the curving counter, and on my right to Cecil Ffrench Salkeld's murals of *Morning* and *Noon*, I come to a less crowded space opposite Gentlemen and Price List, where a bright, glass-walled room opens off to the right. Through the glass I can see the shoppers in Creation Arcade and, at a table this side of the glass, John Ryan sipping burgundy. Now at last I take off my raincoat, fold it and leave it with my plastic bag on the floor against a radiator in the Arcade room, under a marble shelf where some are lunching on high stools. Catching a barman's eyes, I order a glass of burgundy and a gorgonzola sandwich. The BBC film crew are moving around towards the front of the bar, and one of them, a woman, goes over and talks to John Ryan. With glass in one hand and sandwich in the other, I stand with my back to

Evening—I glance at it to make sure it's that, and reflect that some day, more propitious than this, I must try to work out who is Davy Byrne and Shaw, Flann O'Brien and Mícheál Mac Liammóir, and all the other worthies who are reputedly to be found in Ffrench Salkeld's idylls. Draught Beers, I note, whether Stout or Ale, cost £1.55. Bottled, they are £1.00 and £1.05 respectively. Half Spirits, whether whiskey or vodka, are £1.35, and Soft Drinks, 80p. My eyes meet those of a bearded man.

—I'm just deciding, I say, that you are not Rodney Rice of RTE.

—I've never been mistaken for him before, he says, but several people have thought I was J.P. Donleavy. And to tell you the truth, I'd prefer that mistake. I'm Brian Malone and this—motioning to the man next to him—is Michael Condellan.

—Some crowd, I say. Bloomsday's blooming.

—I've been at it, he says, since breakfast in the Tower in Sandycove this morning. I know nothing about Joyce but I go along there every year.

—Who's that, I ask, the man dressed up like Joyce?

—Jim Carroll, says Brian. He does it every year.

I say he's the spitting image, and he is—complete with spectacles, moustache and striped blazer. We talk for a while, and then I go over and speak to John Ryan.

—Hard at it? I say. Have the BBC roped you in?

—I've been at it since breakfast in the Tower, he says. I did a spiel for them there on Joyce. They want me with them all day.

—I'm very sorry, I say, you didn't come to the Zagreb conference anyhow, even if they did make a mess of inviting you. They had your name on the printed programme. You heard that Mira Buljan phoned you from their Writers' Union club and spoke to your son? I was with her. Tell him to come now, today, we expect him, she said. She was very sorry not to be able to show you her island.

—Yes, I heard they phoned, he said. Ach sure I couldn't just get up and go like that. These things must be arranged.

—It was good, I say, especially the Adriatic part.

On the walls there are framed paintings of Leopold Bloom's adventures. The BBC woman comes over and talks to him again. Rosemary Wilton.

—We'd like you sitting over in the front part, she says.

And to me:

—Come with him.

She asks us what we'd like to drink and goes off. Moving in the general direction she has indicated, I find myself talking to Jim Carroll.

—You know who I'm missing terribly? he says. John Jordan. He would be here. He was always here.

We talk about John's death during the Cumann Merriman visit to Cardiff.

—I've heard different versions, I say. What did happen?

—He was choked by a ham sandwich which someone brought to him in his bedroom. As ridiculous as that. A friend of mine was once nearly choked by a pea that went down the wrong way. He went all blue in the face, it was frightening, but I gave him a slap on the back in time.

I move forward again and Rosemary Wilton is pointing to a table at the end of the bar, facing the entrance. There are two glasses of burgundy on it. Soon John ambles over and joins me. Colin Henderson turns up.

—I thought I might be missing the crack, he says, and sits down beside us.

Bláithín de Sachy, who manages the Hendricks Gallery, comes in with a man and they sit down and order lunch. The film crew are endlessly arranging cameras. Gerald Davis appears in bowler hat, black suit, red carnation, the epitome of Bloom, Jew, Dubliner. In the crowd between the counter and the murals, someone, a young man, starts giving a reading from *Ulysses* which we cannot hear. But the TV people are there recording it. John Ryan sits placid beside me, drinking, looking at the Contents page of the *New York Review of Books*. There is an article on "The Scandal of *Ulysses*" and a review of *Nora: The Real Life of Molly Bloom*, the new book by Brenda Maddox.

—Let me see what the "scandal" is, I say.

He hands me the paper and I find it's the new, corrected edition of *Ulysses*. The writer, John Kidd of the University of Virginia, is furious about *Ulysses: The Corrected Text* (1986), prepared by Hans Walter Gabler of the University of Munich, with the help of two graduate students, Wolfhard Steppe and Claus Melchior. It appears that, in the copies of *Ulysses* now on the market, this text has replaced all others; and, if we are to believe Professor Kidd, it is full of absurdities. For example, he cites two real-life Dubliners of 1904 who were mentioned in the book, Harry Thrift and Captain Buller, whose names have now been "corrected" to Shrift and Culler, respectively. The new version "differs radically from what Joyce himself brought forth in 1922 and approved again in 1926, 1932, 1935, and 1936". During Joyce's life, John Kidd says, "hundreds of typographical errors in the first edition were corrected, but a similar number of new variants slipped in unnoticed in later editions, meaning that the first and last lifetime texts were equally distant from what Joyce intended. Suddenly, in the 1980s we were told that there were 'thousands' of errors all along, at least seven on every page. That claim is a sales pitch for the new edition, and has no basis in the texts themselves. *Ulysses: The Corrected Text* is not a purified text (new blunders like 'Shrift' aside), but a different version from what Joyce conceived, authorized, and saw into print."

I can see that part of Kidd's worry is about scholarly edifices that have been built on the text(s) now displaced, and I recall Bruce Arnold talking about the flights of Yeats scholarship. But what strikes me with a shock is that printing, as a technique, does not seem to have improved all that much on handwriting as a means of transmitting a text. Whole passages of his article remind me of the learned commentaries on particular words or phrases in critical editions of Homer or Catullus.

At 2.15 on the clock, I take my leave of John and Colin.

—See you in the Ormond, I say.

Colin replies that he won't be there, he has to interview Denis Donoghue. Recovering my coat and bag, I exit onto Duke Street and turn right in the general direction of the National Museum and Library. In front of the pub and along the street there is an air of gaiety. A couple in Edwardian clothes cycle past on a tandem. From Barrie's, men's outfitters, I cross Duke Lane to Burgess of the same trade. Up the lane, all the other men's shops. Alias Thom's, where I fitted myself out splendidly when I won the prize at the posh dinner in the Shelbourne for starving Ethiopia. John Miller, Medalist is above Ladbrokes, the bookies. There are art galleries and Pat Crowley's boutique. Why do I still remember that, at Terry Keane's party in Killiney ten years ago, I told Pat I'd visit her there? Because I dislike breaking my word.

At Aquascutum of London, elegant clothiers, I turn right into airy, affluent Dawson Street and count two steps up to the pretty Tea Time Express cake-shop where Connellan used sell his proselytising books. In the window of Jackson-Stops & McCabe's, Estate Agents, coloured pictures of houses turn on perpendicular spits. No, I remind myself—I still do—I am not coming to the Royal Hibernian Hotel, which once formed with the Russell and the Shelbourne a glorious trio in these parts. Instead, and it is at least a decorous replacement, there is this off-white office building that houses the Royal Hibernian Shopping Way leading through to Grafton Street. At its entrance, a flower-shop, Molly Blooms, with a card in the window wishing me "Happy Bloomsday". A group of sandwich-boys and girls in the white and black uniforms of the Dublin Sandwich Board Company come towards me carrying placards. "Visit Bewley's on Bloomsday". I have read somewhere that Bewley's have "events" all day: a "breakfast" and a Junior James Joyce Lookalike Competition and the poet Brendan Kennelly reading. They stand at the entrance to the Hibernian Way, smiling and chatting. The blue litter-bin beside me is freshly painted. LITTER, and beneath it, BRÚSCAR, look good in yellow with the blue. They're usually white. Between them the city's coat of arms, and for the first time I actually read its motto: *Obedientia Civium Urbis Felicitas. Obedientia* shocks, an unfashionable word, and even more that it should be the city's official recipe for civic happiness. Strange that as democracy came in, the people supposedly ruling themselves, *obedience* to government became irksome. Or is that only in some countries, such as this postcolonial, anarchic one? Not far from the litter-bin an erect board on the footpath invites me to "walk back a thousand years" on a Millennium Walking Tour AD988-1988. "Unique way to discover a thousand years of Dublin life. Commencing at the following times". But we know by now, with all this talk the Millennium has brought us about Dublin's history—and some of us even learned it in school—that Dublin was founded in 841, not 988. And we know that the Corporation thought up the Millennium because it wanted to "boost the citizens' morale", damaged by all the dereliction and lawlessness, and because Galway had a Quincentennial two years ago, and Cork an Octocentennial last year. The Bewley's sandwich people move off into the Hibernian Way. Terry Keane comes quickly down the street, catches my eye, calls "Sorry, Desmond, I'm flying", and disappears into the Hibernian Way. She must be heading for an appointment in the trendy Buttery Brasserie. Terry's definition of "a trendy place"—"where I go". The Brasserie commemorates by its name—the Buttery part—

the famous bar in the basement of the Hibernian Hotel, which Douglas Gageby often lunched in when he was editor of the *Irish Times*. He told me, when we lunched there once—why do I remember gins and tonic and particularly the thin lemon slices, are they a symbol of the lightness of the ambiance?—that it was one of his favourite places.

Across the street, in two new buildings of dark red brick, the Standard Chartered and Hong Kong Banks frame Molesworth Street. I cross to its left-hand side and then to the other. This sombre, respectable, Protestant street has become, since the natives took over, a political street. At its further end, framed in its T-junction with Kildare Street, Leinster House, the nation's parliament, behind trees and high railings, the gardaí on duty in their box. As I move, the new red-brick buildings have become the Government Publications Office with colourful children's books in Gaelic in the window, and on this side the offices of the European Parliament and the EC Commission, Coimisiún na gComhphobal Eorpach. At the corner of this lane, where signs indicate three art galleries, is a strangely antique, unilingual sign, "Molesworth Place 1831" in gold letters, rescued, it seems, from an older wall and set into this re-built one. Old houses now with railings around basement areas. The Registry Office, where, if you are in a hurry or wish to disown religion, you can marry without church ceremony. Ray Crotty, deep in thought, comes striding along the far side. Ray who held up Europe by challenging the Single European Act in the courts and forcing the Government to hold a referendum. He's probably coming from his office in Trinity. The Protestant Orphan Society, and across from it, under the sign of the compass and set square, the grand pillared and balconied building of the Grand Order of Freemasons. As I approach Buswell's Hotel, where I go on the first Wednesday of each month for a meeting of the Constitution Club, which I founded two years ago with

Crotty and five other would-be reformers of the state, it occurs to me that perhaps Jim Gorry from Gorry's Gallery might accompany me tonight from Holles Street on. So I cross and enter the doorway of the house and continue along a corridor into the gallery, where they show splendid Irish paintings of the nineteenth and early twentieth centuries, and find his wife, Thérèse there and tell her my story.

—He's probably in Cunningham's café around the corner on Kildare Street, she says. Go and ask himself. He has a bit of a cold, but he might be on for it.

The Tricolour is flying over Leinster House, prototype of Washington's White House. Didn't I read in Maurice Craig's book on Dublin that when the Duke of Leinster built it here, unfashionably, sometime in the mid-eighteenth century, he said "They'll follow me here", meaning from the fashionable Northside, and they did? To either side of it, facing each other across the railinged car-park, the National Library and National Museum, in sombre grey stone, massive and sculptural with pillars and rotundas, form an architectural cluster out of ancient Rome or modern Washington. High on the wall at the corner of Molesworth Street, the street-sign still reads *Sráid Teach Laibhean*. If it were *Laighean*, it would mean what it's supposed to mean—"Leinster House Street", the name of Molesworth Street in Gaelic—but as it is, it means Lavan House Street, that is to say, nothing intelligible. Four years ago I wrote about it in my column in the *Sunday Press*, and later I sent a letter about it to the *Irish Times*. It is not that a mistake in the Gaelic form of a street-name is unusual—far from it—but I felt that at the very least where the Deputies and Senators and Ministers pass in and out daily on the nation's business, decorum required some care for literacy in what the Constitution calls "the first official language". But it stands there still, a symbol not only of that particular sham, but of the much deeper not-caring that infects the Republic mortally.

I turn right into Kildare Street, enter Cunningham's little café, and Jim is sitting there with his daughter.

—Hello, Jim, I say. Thérèse said you'd be here. I'm doing a Bloomsday walk around the town and I was wondering would you like to join me at Holles Street Hospital at 9.45 and do the last bit with me, nighttown and all that, and end up in Joys.

—What's Joys? asks Jim, and I tell him a night-club on Baggot Street.

—Well, I'd love to, he says, but I was thinking of an early night. I've been feeling tired and I've a bit of a cold. Will you have a coffee?

—No, thanks, I say, duty calls. I'm due in the Museum by now. Thérèse told me you weren't your best, but maybe what you need to restore you is a vigorous adventure.

—Maybe you're right, he says, and smiles. I tell you, I'll see. If I feel up to it, I'll be there. Where—at the Hospital? A quarter to ten?

—Yes, just inside the front door.

—Anyway thanks for asking me, he says.

I smile at his daughter, wave to both of them, cross to the National Museum, pass through its narrow gate, and after a few paces mount four steps that bring me into the semicircular portico. Then, traversing the circular hall past attendants attending and counters offering cards and books, I turn right and enter the Treasury, as they call the rooms where they gathered together all the most precious objects from the Irish Golden Age after they had returned from their tour in America and Europe. A man at a table takes a pound, and I see over there in a glass case the lovely little gold boat with seats and mast and oars from 100 BC or thereabouts which was found with a hoard of precious things in County Derry. Wait now. I expected much later stuff. There is an explanatory card about the Celts, and on another card I see from a diagram that this room and the adjoining part of the next, very long room are "Pagan Iron Age". Then comes the Golden Age. Very well, maybe that travelling exhibition had more than Golden Age things, or I was mistaken about this permanent exhibition being a continuation of it. Through the door into the big room I see movement into a curtained-off area for a video showing. A man's voice starts to speak there, echoingly, and I recognise it as Andy O'Mahony whom I have listened to for more than twenty years on RTE radio. I move into the big room to a glass case showing bronze box-lids from the first century AD.

Soft music of a "Celtic", Ó Riada kind sounds behind Andy's voice. He is saying, boomingly, through the curtain:

—By the time history began in the fifth century, Ireland had seen seven thousand years of human settlement.

The music takes over. With my mind's eye I see vast land-scapes and remains of human settlement. I switch on the recorder.

—We know that the society which was first recorded in any detail in the fifth century AD was rural. There were no towns, no villages and no coinage. Agriculture was the mainstay of the economy, and cattle-raising—celebrated in ancient sagas—was important. The people spoke the fore-runner of modern Irish. The poet and the skilled craftsman were honoured. There were many small tribal kingdoms grouped under more powerful kings who vied with each other for dominance. The kings of Tara and Cashel enjoyed special eminence. We don't know when a Celtic language was first spoken in Ireland, nor do we know how such a language came to be introduced, whether by peaceful settlement, military conquest or by other means. What we *can* say is that objects which on mainland Europe were associated with Celtic-speaking people began to appear in Ireland from the seventh century BC onwards.

This is very good, very carefully done. "All the latest scholarship" deftly summarised.

—In the third century BC a golden collar was imported into Ireland. It was decorated with a simple version of the art style known as La Tène after a Celtic site of that name in Switzerland. This style, characterised by curved lines, scrolls and spirals, became rooted in Ireland and survived here for many centuries. It lasted to become a major element in the Christian art of the early medieval period, generally known as the Golden Age. In the first century AD the Romans invaded Britain and rapidly brought most of the island under their control. Ireland traded with the Empire and received new technical and artistic ideas. By the fourth century the Empire was in decline in the West and Britain was often raided by the Irish.

Well, by the Gaels really. Even the word Irish didn't exist then in any form. The Gaels were the predecessor nation of the Irish, related to us as spiritual, and to a certain extent physical, ancestors, as the Hebrews are related to the Jews.

—Amongst the plunder they brought back was the slave boy, Patrick. He was later to be remembered as the principal apostle of Ireland.

"Remembered as"—subtle wording, all the latest scholarship again.

—It was with Patrick that Irish history really began, because he left us in his writings a vivid picture of the life of a missionary in a turbulent society. Into this traditional society Christianity came as a breath of fresh air. It offered new outlets to talented people. It placed demands on craftsmen for new kinds of objects—altar vessels and reliquaries. It introduced the new art of writing texts—

Very good, not *writing*, that had been done in Ogham as inscriptions on stones.

—and the new architecture for church buildings, and above all it gave a new meaning to work, especially fine craftsmanship, which became a form of prayer.

Music takes over. What "fine craftsmanship" are they showing?

—The Irish church was established by bishop missionaries from Britain and Gaul. Sometime in the later fifth or early sixth century, monasticism was introduced to Ireland and it proved to be very popular.

Yes, indeed, the bishops faded into the background, tended their cattle, hoed their plots, were called on when needed for confirmations—and ordinations?

—This was partly because the family nature of monasteries was attractive to the Irish. The sixth century seems to have been a great period for founding monasteries. Some monasteries grew to great wealth and importance and in later centuries built large churches and erected high crosses, many of which survive today.

Music. Ah, the high crosses! Moone, Monasterboice, lovely, towering, solid, delicate, sculpture-encrusted things!

—The metalwork which survives from the early period is simple. Our earliest manuscript dates from about 600 AD and it too is simply decorated. By the end of the sixth century, Irish monks were themselves undertaking missionary work. St Colmcille of Iona and St Aedan of Lindisfarne, St Columbanus at Luxeuil in Gaul and later at Bobbio in northern Italy. St Gall at Sankt Gallen in what is now Switzerland, and St Cilian at Würzburg—and many others. Through the monasteries which they founded, profound European influences came into Irish art. The Christian art of early medieval Ireland drew heavily on the craftsmanship of earlier times. The La Tène style of the Iron Age survived. In the seventh and eighth centuries, animals, sometimes inter-laced, sometimes more or less lifelike, became a dominant theme. These came to Irish art from two sources—the naturalistic ones from the early Christian art of the Mediter-ranean world and Gaul, and the interlaced motifs from the animal art of the Germanic tribes which overwhelmed the Roman Empire. Interlace appears in Irish art about this time, and it too can be traced to the Mediterranean world. All of these traditions come together in the Book of Durrow, a seventh-century gospel book. Painting reached perfection in the late eighth century in the Book of Kells.

Music, as they show those pages into which you look, and look, and get lost in the intricacy, so that your head swims and you begin to feel giddy and swoon.

—Much of the painting in manuscripts seems to be based on the work of the goldsmith and the bronzesmith, and it is in their work that most of the best work of the time is preserved. The eighth and early ninth centuries seem to have been the period of greatest creativity. The Ardagh Chalice and Derrynaflan paten show the style off with marvellous artistry. Patterns, some abstract, some naturalistic, are executed with a breathtaking range of techniques—multi-coloured enamels, engraving, knitted wire mesh, stamped foils, and gold filigree of great complexity and refinement.

I have moved to a case where "trial pieces" are shown—flat pieces of bone on which the designer-craftsman sketched his designs and patterns. Themselves little works of art, shockingly moving as they bring you right back beside that thinking, executing man who did this all that time ago. No one speaks of their tools. What were they? Fine and sure enough to do this.

—Reliquaries were made at this time, as the churches became wealthier and more secure and wished to commemorate their own history. Some of the fine metal work was done for kings and other great personages. Indeed, the history of the brooches gives a good outline of the development of early Irish art. The earliest form is penannular, that is, with a gap in the ring.

I am looking at an explanatory card about Penannular Brooches.

—These were cloak-fastenings and were decorated with red enamel and sometimes little plates of *millefiori*. By the eighth century, a new form, the large and complete ring-brooch, appears. No longer capable of being used for fastening clothes, the head was enlarged to display ornaments. The finest and earliest is the Tara Brooch.

Music. I'll look at it again in a moment.

—Later brooches tend to be simpler. By the ninth century enamel had become less common, but amber remained popular. Engraving and cast-metal embellishments were gradually substituted for the artistry and variety of the best eighth-century work. Filigree became poorer. Apart from brooches, the decline in technical accomplishment can be seen in objects even as ambitious as the Derrynaflan Chalice.

Which the man found in Tipperary a few years ago, using a metal detector, and about which there was a big court-case.

—The monastic culture of Ireland was stable, wealthy, confident, and for its time cosmopolitan. Monasteries traded abroad for raw materials, such as amber, silver and gold. They became great storehouses and in a rural society they seem to have played some of the commercial role of towns. Monasteries became politically powerful, and their abbots ruled them as lay rulers, passing the succession from father to son. The first Viking raids—

An ominous note in the background music.

—began at the close of the eighth century. Their object was plunder—emptying the monasteries of their wealth, and taking prisoners for the European slave market. In the 840s the Vikings began to build permanent fortresses along the coast, from which trading towns such as Dublin, Waterford, Wexford and Limerick grew. Dublin became one of the most important ports on the Viking trade routes, along which exotic products like silks and silver flowed from the Middle East. Silver was used increasingly for ornaments of all kinds during the tenth and eleventh centuries.

Enough, Andy, and thanks.

I move into the centre of the room among the great masterpieces. I search for the Tara Brooch, and as I confront it, it occurs to me that I am "observing" the incipient swooning effect that comes when I peer into the fine filigree. It is preceded, I notice, by a sort of giddy war between the messages from my seeing eyes, on the one hand, and my reason or commonsense judgement on the other. There is a sense, a feeling, that the *existence* of this work, done by a man, is absurd. I recall Giraldus Cambrensis, in his oft-quoted long passage about looking at Irish manuscript paintings in the twelfth century—how he concludes by saying that, as one looks, one gradually comes to the conviction that it has been done "not by men, but by angels". The three or four master-pieces that everyone knows about are not easy to locate. There is no sign saying "Tara Brooch" or "Ardagh Chalice" or "Cross of Cong". One discovers them only as one moves from case to case and reads the small card indicating the nature of the object, place of finding and suchlike. This seems to me a pity. I am disappointed at what seems a mandarin contempt, on the part of the Museum authorities, for the popular namings and the predictable goals of people as they entered this Holy of Holies of ancient Gaelic art. But as I reflect, no; it seems the right way to do it. Let the famous objects be dis-covered in passing, as it were. It is better not to encourage or provoke that mad touristic surge such as makes a bee-line for the Mona Lisa in the Louvre, paying scant attention to all around it.

I leave the Museum and at the gate to Kildare Street read a poster offering, for the Millennium doubtless, a Commemorative Medal of Sitric Silkbeard, King of Dublin, 989-1036 AD, sponsored by the National Museum of Ireland in association with the Bank of Ireland. It was Sitric who introduced coinage to Dyfflin, so the medal is based aptly on one of his coins. The young garda on duty at the Leinster House gate has the fresh looks and smiling eyes of a country lad. That big office-building across the street displays a brass-plate which seems to say Department of Finance, but I know that some members of the Oireachtas have offices in it because I once visited Senator John Robb there.

The approach to the National Library, through a narrow gate and up a few steps, is a replica of that to the Museum. In the circular hall there is an exhibition of "Dublin Delineated—1688-1988". Drawings, photographs, maps and prints. By a flight of steps and, turning left, another flight, I enter the Reading Room, sign the book on the counter, and find all in order. At the numbered tables, some of them with broken lamps, within the round walls filled with reference books, men and women, young and old, sit studiously. I come here seldom, usually to search among the reference books for a dictionary of, say, Old Norse, or an article in an encyclopedia. Behind the counter where the librarian sits pensive, the room where a lanky girl in short leather skirt issued me with a reader's ticket. Beside me a standing man is consulting, on a stand in front of him, a copy of the *Tuam News and Western Advertiser* for September 14, 1888. A woman sitting beside him is leafing through copies of the *Leinster Leader*. All in order. Learning proceeds. I descend the stairs to the circular hall and leave. A party of schoolchildren is standing at the door to Leinster House.

At the gate I turn right towards Nassau Street, heading for Temple Bar.

3.05 - 4.30

KILDARE STREET VIA TEMPLE BAR
TO UPPER ORMOND QUAY

One does not expect to see a crash on staid, one-way Kildare Street, but that is what has happened. It seems the elderly woman with her husband beside her in the Volkswagen came out of Setanta Place and hit the red Fiat coming up from Nassau Street. The young man who was driving it is standing beside it wearing an expression of exasperated patience, looking at his shoes or up and down the street, making no approach to the couple. Evidently he assumes that because the garda at the Leinster House entrance saw the crash, the police will arrive any minute.

A line of tour buses is parked on the other side of Nassau Street under Trinity's wall and high green railing. Trinity's park all along that side makes this a street of one side, not quite a real street. It is pleasant to sit upstairs in The Coffee Bean and look beyond the railing at the trees and grass. The Kilkenny Shop. Ah the sixties, when Ireland, or rather some of the new whizzkids who were making Ireland hum, discovered Scandinavian Design, and declared it the national saviour, and brought Swedes in to tell us that we hadn't much visual sense, and set up the Kilkenny Design Centre in the Butlers' castle in Kilkenny in imitation of the castle full of craft workshops in Fredrikstad near Oslo. It has good things, but dear. My own favourite shop for beautiful things on Nassau Street is the Blarney Woollen Mills. Well, I am thinking especially about clothes, women's clothes. The women's clothes it puts on dummies in the windows would predispose me to love the wearer. I like wool on women. Not that it's all wool, particularly this time of the year. That dummy in the red pullover with big flowers on the breast is wearing a viscose skirt. They have matched that particular red well with that blue-green. They have a good matcher. The dummy beside her has a white blouse with a climbing-rose pattern of pink and light green, a pink cardigan knotted casually around the waist, an umbrella in dark green and dark pink hanging from it, and a light beige linen skirt. They're displaying china with shamrocks on it, which is not my cup of tea. The lace and the embroidered cloths are exquisite. A big blonde woman looking into the window is wearing a red jumper with "Indiana 1987 National Championships' in white. In the doorway of the newsagent's, a headline says "Soviets Snatch Draw with Ireland", and with an eye to the tourists they have the *Frankfurter Allgemeine*, *Figaro, Corriere della Sera* and *New York Herald Tribune*. There's Miranda Healy coming out of Fred Hanna's bookshop with what looks like a book in a bag, and turning towards the corner of Dawson Street. Since the English firm, Waterstone's opened around the corner, directly opposite Hodges Figgis, Dublin's book emporium is hereabouts, within a few hundred square yards. But Waterstone's have upped the ante with their Sunday and late opening, and their blatant new selling style—the books piled in stacks pell mell on tables. Hodges Figgis, that venerable old firm that have sold books since before my childhood, have been forced to imitate or perish. Tourists and students are crossing from Dawson Street into the back maw of the Trinity Arts Block. The big chestnut tree at the entrance to the maw must have stood in the College park before they opened this gap in the wall. On the seat around its bole a tall, blonde boy with a

Swedish flag on his rucksack sits eating an icecream. Beyond Dawson Street, at the Pen Shop, I draw level with Miranda and say hello.

—Oh hello, she says, I thought you were Bloomsdaying.

—I am. I'm on my way to the Ormond. Want to come?

—Isn't that down the quays? she says.

I confirm that it is, not far from the Four Courts.

—There'll be a celebration there around four.

We are at the bottom of Grafton Street, facing into Suffolk Street. The clock on the opposite corner says 3.15.

—That's a brilliant idea, she says. I know nothing about Joyce. I might learn something.

—I'd like the company, I say, but I'll have to ask you to be tolerant of my strange obsession with the things we're passing, and my talking now and then into this gadget. I'm working.

—Work away. I'll tag along. Aren't you hot in that coat?

—It's the easiest way to carry it. You know how the day started out.

Over the buildings on the right-hand side of Suffolk Street I can see the top of the Central Bank and the ugly tangle of great girders on the roof. People would not see that if Sam Stephenson had been allowed to have his way and crown the building with a resplendent copper covering. But the floors, or rather, the ducts and pipes they contained, had taken up more space than he had reckoned for, so that the finished building would be 32 feet higher than the planning permission allowed, and leaving the roof uncovered was the compromise which the Minister ordained. We cross into Suffolk Street, closed at the further end by the fine edifice of the National Irish Bank whose title always makes me smile. By a fluke—it was Con Howard who asked me, he has connections everywhere—I was at its inaugural reception when the *Australian* bank which owns it gave it that name in place of "the Northern Bank". Half-way up the spire of St Andrew's, part of a telecommunications dish on some roof further back protrudes sinisterly, like a great ear. The Paperback Centre has closed. First casualty of Waterstone's onslaught. In the empty window there are posters about books by James Joyce and Seamus Heaney, and one about Milan Kundera's *Unbear-able Lightness of Being*. Enquiries to the branch in the Stillorgan Shopping Centre.

—Have you read that, asks Miranda, *The Unbearable Lightness of Being*? I was looking for it in Hanna's but they didn't have it in stock.

—No, I say, I was afraid from the title that it would be full of vapid Slav philosophising. I'm always wary of these hyped books by "dissidents".

—From what I hear, it's a love story. It's supposed to be very good.

Combridge's Art Gallery. Modern art and all its movements have come and gone and Combridge's pictures have shown no sign of it. Always those placid seascapes, harbours and mountains, and those portraits of fiery gypsy girls.

—What did you get in Hanna's? I ask her.

O'Neill's big, hectic pub, at the corner among the banks. Trinity students make a noise there, Brendan Kennelly holds court, and I met Terence Brown there for a deep discussion after we had returned from the great symposium on a "Project for Ireland" which Pat Sheeran and Nina Witoszek convened in Galway.

—*Rates of Exchange* by Malcolm Bradbury, she says, and a book about France.

We stop at the St Andrew's spire, just short of the curve leading to that cluster of good restaurants where the Trocadero is my favourite.

—When are you off? I ask.

—Next week. I'm joining the circus in Lyons next Thursday.

Miranda is a fire-eater.

We cross to O'Neill's and continue down little Church Lane, jam-packed with cars and buses waiting to disgorge into financial Dame Street. I remember a prim Protestant schoolteacher in Kinsale who amazed me when she told me she spent her summers with a circus. But when she said she looked after the horses it fitted. In the middle of Dame Street, Eddie Delaney's massy Thomas Davis looks over the head of Grattan at Trinity's blue clock. His great-coat, very Delaney this, dissolves into gobs of metal drooping down his lower back.

Left now for a few yards until we can just see the waterfall in front of the Central Bank, and then across Dame Street into Anglesea Street, Sráid Mhóna.

Móna. Sometime I must really clear up this business of calling Anglesey Móna, when it is a fact that Caesar, in his description of Britain, wrote clearly, "In hoc medio cursu"— referring to the Irish Sea and saying "half-way across it"— "est insula quae appellatur Mona". That is obviously, and is taken to be, the Isle of Man. And it tallies with the fact that it was indeed called in Irish Mana, pronounced Monna, or Mon-a with a short o. True, Tacitus later referred to Anglesey as Mona, and I've heard that the Welsh call it Mon with a long o, which leaves Irish little choice. But I suspect there is some ancient confusion at work there. These old streets of warehouses, solicitors and accountants, from here to the Liffey, have come to be known as "the Temple Bar area", "Dublin's Left Bank" as the papers say, since CIE bought up whole streets with a view to demolishing them and building a big bus station, and in the interim rented out premises at low rents on short leases. It has many artists' studios, recording studios, practising studios, the Project Arts Centre where the Rough Magic company are the stars, the Film Institute and Claddagh Records and the Alchemist's Head science fiction bookshop, the Eager Beaver and American Classics second-hand clothes shops, and Rudyard's, the Bad

Ass Café, the Pigalle and the Bridge Café, to name but a few of its many cafés and restaurants. This girl bobbing along in front of us in short black skirt and with long blonde hair is the kind of girl you'd expect to see here. I can imagine her red cherry-lips in a white face. Yesterdays red bar seems to be attached to Bloom's Hotel.

—Excuse me a moment, Miranda, I say, while I investigate this place.

I am interested in it because of its name, but I also want to pee. In the foyer I see that Yesterday's Bar—as it's written here—is an annexe, but it is closed for the holy hour. No jacks in sight. I go upstairs to the Trinity Room Restaurant which looks empty through the glass door. No sign of the Bloom theme continuing. A waiter with tray emerges through the glass door and asks, officiously, "Can I help you, sir?", and I say "No thank you", and continue up steps which lead onto a corridor with bedrooms. But still no jacks in sight. Frustrated, I return to the street, to Miranda standing in a patch of sun under a Bureau de Change sign of Allied Irish Banks.

—You see that street there, Cope Street, I say. When I was a boy, Cope Street meant where Dada went to work, and earned our daily bread laboriously as we were continually informed. It meant specifically No. 6, there where Coffer's restaurant is now. He had a wholesale grocery business. It was funny having lunch there with Conor Brady shortly after he became editor of the *Irish Times*, in the very room which used to be the front office, and where my father's faithful, all-enduring slave, Miss Ennis, used sit at her desk. Nolan's there, a few doors away, was his great rival.

Across the street, on the brick wall of USIT, the students' travel agency, we read across the street "Love the Horde 'cos you're gonna to die", and crossing from the Stock Exchange to inspect more closely read "Emma, Maura, Ashling, Clodagh". USIT offers Paris £49.50 one way plus £5 tax. At the corner where Anglesea Street meets Fleet Street coming from the right, I enter the Anna Livia pub, which has a Plurabelle Lounge upstairs, and passing red plush seats descend a red-carpeted stairs to a blue lavatory which meets my need. *Abha*, silent *b*, is river. *Abha na Lif-e*, the River Liffey. Anna Livia is a play on that. Back in the bar I find Miranda standing beside the hot-plate where a chef is surveying the remains of lunch in his pots.

—They've got coddle, she says, have you ever eaten that?

—No, I say, looking in the pot and descrying a sort of creamy stew. I'm tempted, but they'll have something equally genuine Dublin at the Ormond I'm sure. I mean Mr Bloom's own dinner of inner organs. And that I must eat today. Are you dying with hunger?

—A bit, but I can wait, she says. Keep to your programme. It's fun.

Outside again, we confront Bedford Row leading on to the Liffey quay. Patrick Cleere, Shooting and Fishing, has his sign there. Perhaps the food in the Pizzeria Italia tastes so good because the place is so small and you can see and smell the food being cooked. Gets the gastric juices working. This maze of little streets is Dublin as it used to be before the Wide Street Commissioners got to work in the late eighteenth century. Fleet Street, continuing straight into Temple Bar and beyond, marks the old shoreline of the Liffey before the quays were built.

We proceed into Temple Bar. Woolcox, Jozeau (Ireland) Ltd Wholesale Chemists looks very ancient. Looks like one of the "solid old firms" with drab, money-making premises that were typical of these streets, and that raised fine Victorian mansions in the suburbs. It is frustrating trying to teach students the proper use of the apostrophe in English when you see it so often omitted in public signs like that there, Rorys (*sic*) Fishing Tackle, on the corner of no, not again, Asdills Row. Not to mention the "intrusive apostrophe", in places where it should not be, which was so frequent in Feargal Quinn's shops that he offered a free bottle of wine to any customer who spotted one. The trades still cluster as in the old days. Hereabouts, from Bedford Row to Parliament Street, it is fishing and shooting.

—This now, I say to Miranda, is the sight that for me gives Temple Bar its buzz.

A stream of shoppers in the sunlight is descending from Dame Street by the side of the Central Bank, and down Crown Alley past the second-hand clothes shops, Rudyard's, the Bad Ass Café, and the old telephone exchange here at the corner, to the cluster of little shops in Merchant's Arch and past them, under the Arch, to the Ha'penny Bridge and beyond. All lightness, colour and movement. Behind this, the hoisted grey rectangle of the Central Bank standing on a narrower rectangular stump like the base of a tree, and with eight slim bands of glass signalling its storeys.

—Yes, she says, I like here. I like wandering here.

At the entrance to the Arch passage, beneath the Vintage Posters and Magazines Shop of Dublin, the Ha'penny Bridge Bookshop where I must buy a book.

—I must buy a book here, I say, and we enter.

Looking along a shelf of books bound in paper, I read *Por Siempre Ambar* Kathleen Winsor, *Chacal* Frederick Forsyth, *La Rosa de Jerico* Frank G. Slaughter, and for a moment have a sense of dislocation or dreaming, of there being some mistake. Then I see that there only five or six books in Spanish.

—Indeed, I say to Miranda, I must buy a book for a woman I cherish, and fate has decreed that it will be you, and that the book, if he has it, will be—

A thin, balding man with a small moustache, wearing glasses, has emerged from a doorway in the corner of the one-room shop.

—Kundera", I say to him, *The Unbearable Lightness of Being.*

Miranda smiles.

—Do you think he'll have it? They all look second-hand to me.

He goes to a shelf, extracts a book and hands it to me. Inside the front cover is written £2.55. On the back it says £3.95, which is sterling because it is published in England. It looks new. It must be a reviewer's copy. Opening it at random, I read :

When Tereza unexpectedly came to visit Tomas in Prague, he made love to her, as I pointed out in Part One, that very day, or rather, that very hour, but suddenly thereafter she became feverish.

—You seem to be right, I say, showing her the sentence.

I buy it and give it to her, and she kisses me on the cheek.

—Watch yourself now, I say, or you'll be shocking my readers.

We leave the shop and walk a short distance between two car-parks to the Temple Bar Gallery in the ground floor of a hugely ugly building that has thirty or so painter's studios. Rusty wire netting on the front of the gallery adds to the grim effect. On the footpath a girl in dungarees, her hair in a bun, has her arms around the neck of a boy in a red and white pullover and they are kissing happily. The Simon Community are to have an exhibition opening here today, but I see by glancing inside that it is still in preparation. There are about thirty dreary-looking paintings on the walls and a young man is fixing up another. "It'll be opening at 6.30", he says. A double-decker bus comes incongruously up the narrow street towards us, almost filling the entire width, just managing to skim by the few cars which, regardless of the double yellow lines, are parked at intervals.

Past a barber's on the corner we enter the Merchant's Arch passage. Here are trinkets, badges, bangles and studded black belts, sun-glasses and espadrilles, black leather jackets with large, white metal zips. This is The Body Merchant Cosmetique, and there in American Classics you can get Jeans, Suedes and Accessories. The trilling of a tin-whistle resounds in the passage. The young man playing it stands in the arch, an upturned cap with a dozen coins in front of him. A dark-skinned man from the Middle East hears nothing of it as he passes, eyes straight ahead, ears plugged into his Walkman. Down steps now to the footpath of Wellington Quay where a traffic-light allows three girls in wine-red school blazers to cross to the Ha'penny Bridge. Then the traffic is released, like bulls for a race, and the roar resumes. When I was living in Connemara and visited Dublin occasionally, it was that roar, so seemingly intolerable, incredible, absurd—how do people live with this?—which used strike me most. On the far quay, by contrast, a long, laden trailer-lorry moves silently as a ship towards O'Connell Bridge. Along both quay walls, at intervals of about sixty yards, there are pairs of metal flagpoles with a lamp on a post between them. Flags are flying from the poles. Scrutinising their colours for significance, I read "tourist season? Millennium?" and wonder have I missed something. Celebration, or rather the signs and symbols of it, which by right should be attached to dates and occasions of shared meaning, have gone terribly awry in Dublin. Knowing that a city should occasionally have them, and a capital city all the more, the Corporation goes through the motions according to some pattern or calendar of its own. For some years now it has put on a "street carnival". I think it's in July. It happens, the children enjoy it, the adults look on. Why *then*, whenever that is, no one knows. I have seen cities celebrate their special days—local, regional, national, civic or religious. Dublin has no day when it consciously celebrates either itself or the nation or the works of God. Dubliners and Irish, we have lost, if we ever had it, the ability to do that. We gape at others doing it—nations, cities—like homeless children wandering the streets at Christmas, looking through windows at the self-possessed.

We turn left past the Dublin Woollen Mills and the Ophthalmic Optician T.P. Cronan.

—Now, Miranda, for the fun of it, will you count how many of these guys there are on the quay.

We cross narrow, cobbled Fownes Street.

—Well, there's another, she says, H. Grant Ophthalmic Optician. That's two.

The Gallery of Photography is showing photographs of Jamaica by Peter Butler. Seventeen minutes to four. The Gold Cup race will be starting in two minutes.

—Three, says Miranda. Alan Fitzpatrick Ophthalmic Optician.

In the window, "Soft Contact Lenses from £125. VDU Tests. Driving Sight Tests. Repairs", and there are pictures of girls looking sophisticated in glasses, and glasses hanging from a trellis among paper flowers. A couple of dead houses and then No. 30, a dark shop called Curios, such as one finds on these quays, or used find. The Open sign on the door is surprising. Through the rusty wire shutter and the encrusted murk of the window I see old coach lamps, an ancient camera, a kneeling Chinese porcelain figure, Victorian table lamps. Behind these in the gloom someone is moving.

—Will we count him? asks Miranda ahead of me. Contact Lens Practitioner, nameless. Four? And there's E. Little FAOI Optometrist. Oh it's the same man. He has two windows.

Across the river, on Lower Ormond Quay, there are jagged gaps among the houses. P.K. Joyce Demolition Excavation is at work there too. Further along, among more semi-ruins, a large poster on a hoarding says "Inner City £ess Taxing".

—Five, says Miranda. "Daniel J. Casey FBOA, Ophthalmic Optician." There's a whole tribe of them, isn't there? Why here?

—Why not, I suppose. But I take your point. There must be a story behind it.

Arnold's Vetinerary offers Newest Sensation, Frisbee Floppy Flying Discs for Dogs. Chains, leads, brushes, books with happy dogs' faces on the covers. We cross Eustace Street. Parked cars make me notice the parking meters, surprising on this busy road. People fall into the river now and then. Those pairs of iron spikes with spherical grips, sticking up at intervals from the quay wall, show where the ladders are to rescue them. Good to know. In front of the office block of Dublin Corporation, at Nos 16-19, the footpath widens so much that four cars are parked on it. This is the bus stop for Routes 21a, 24, 51, 51B, 51C, 68, 69, 78. 78A, 78B, 79 and 90. A woman in a blue windbreaker is leaning on the litter-bin attached to the metal post. On the shelter, among the many scribbles, Corinna, Rona, Sharon, Jackie, The Communards. We have come to Bassi's which has two big windows. Slender, oval Virgins, Gabriel the Archangel, Childs of Prague. A picture of Jesus as the Sacred Heart and another with his hands clasped together under his nose, deep in thought. After the convulsions in sacred art which followed the Second Vatican Council, they are surprisingly traditional. The main concession to modern fashion seems to be an elongation, a certain "slimming", in the statues. Selling into the mass market of church furnishings and religious houses, Bassi cannot afford more.

—Do you know, Miranda, slimming is the hankering after spirit of a materialist world, its substitute for spirituality. The less body, the better the person. The more refined, it is believed.

—Oh I know your thing about that, at least where women are concerned. The more the better.

—Well, within limits, yes, especially if I'm fond of her. The more of her the better.

Roger Greene and Son, Commissioner for Oaths, is at No. 11, the third of three solicitors in a row. *Cumann Oib-*

ridhe Bhaile Átha Cliath, The Dublin Working Men's Club, is in the old Gaelic script that I learned at school. Instead of those aspirating *h*'s which go with the Roman script, a dot, or *buailte* as we used say, on the preceding consonant. You don't often see it now. Coming up to the Clarence Hotel the line of parked cars is unbroken. Audi, five Toyotas— some Carina or Corolla, one Celica—Opel Kadett, Mazda, Mitsubishi, Vauxhall.

—Oh that's the Ormond there now, the creamy-white building, says Miranda, pointing ahead across the river, beyond Grattan Bridge. I've seen it before, but without ever really noticing it.

—I know it, I say, as the place where you get one of the private buses to Tuam. It's their halting spot.

Further upriver the green and grey dome of the Four Courts shows above the rooftops. Here, this side of the bridge, the river Poddle entered the Liffey—and probably still does underground for all that I know—and a short distance up its estuary was the *Dubhlinn* or black pool that gave Dublin its name. Well, in every language except Irish: *Baile Átha Cliath*, Town of the Hurdleford, on the Dublin Working Men's Club. Black, *deep* pool—that was what interested the Vikings, an anchorage, and here they built their town which remained the core of the city for centuries. They founded it in 841. The Corporation, wanting a Millennium, chose to commemorate, not the founding, but the date when the well-founded Viking town of Dyfflin was taken and taxed by an Irish king. But even then, I have read, the Millennium is out by a year and should be next year. The year 988 was taken from the Annals of Ulster, which are out by a year until 1014. Their 988 was really 989. We are standing at the corner where Parliament Street meets Wellington Quay and receives the traffic from the bridge and Capel Street. Miranda is staring at the coloured friezes which run around the noble, neglected building on the opposite corner.

—They're supposed to represent the processes of soap-making, I say. You see the various figures doing this and that like in one of those old Egyptian paintings. And look, there's Sunlight Chambers over the door. So presumably the building once belonged to Sunlight Soap. Listen, I'm thinking. You see that bookie's up the street there? Let's go and find out who won the Ascot Gold Cup. It's part of the ritual.

We cross to the other footpath, pass a few houses and enter Hackett's Betting Office on the corner of Essex Gate. Nine or ten men are watching the television set in the corner, and two girls can be seen seated behind bars at the end of the room. A man is writing on printed lists of runners on the wall.

—I suppose, I say to him, the Gold Cup's over. What won it?

—Royal Gait was first past the post, but he was disqualified. The winner was Sadeem.

The *Independent*, quoting a TV tip for Primitive Rising, added "Danger— Sadeem." The dark horse.

—What about Primitive Rising?

—Didn't figure.

We return to the corner and cross to Grattan Bridge, which everyone calls Capel Street Bridge, and which for centuries was Essex Bridge. The old Custom House stood here. This was the anchorage. The lamp pillars on the green iron balustrades are supported by pairs of seahorses. A welcome fresh breeze blows from the sea. Down there where it comes from, Liberty Hall and the tall white building with the Sony ad stand highest on the skyline, and the, shall we say, *new* Custom House is dwarfed between them. Ahead of us, framed between Harty Newsagent and the Bank of Ireland, old Capel Street runs straight as a die. The best street in Dublin, Joyce called it, and I would come near to agreeing with him. A no-nonsense, good-value commercial street, it reminds me of streets, off-centre, in Madrid, Paris or

Vienna which you see from buses or trams as you pass. Good for hiking gear, house fittings, hardware. Gerald Davis has his gallery there and Slattery's is good for music. Along Ormond Quay lorries and buses, two abreast, are braying infernally.

Then the lights release the flow from Capel Street and we cross to the Bank of Ireland and in a few steps reach the Ormond, which is bedecked with the flags of the nations. A round plaque on its wall says: "The Ormond Hotel is the setting for the episode THE SIRENS in Joyce's *Ulysses*". Across the river, two windowless houses, Adam and Eve's church, and the twin towers of Sam Stephenson's Civic Offices, a bit of Christ Church showing behind them.

—Miranda, have you any idea why that Franciscan church is called Adam and Eve's?

—Wasn't there a pub there in the old days that was called that? That's what I heard.

No wonder Sam Stephenson's gone to London. People say how awful his Civic Offices look, but they're not finished, he says; there are meant to be four towers. "Judging them as they are", he said, "is like catching a man with his pants down". Like his Central Bank with its girders showing.

We enter the Ormond. On the right, in Malachi O'Flynn's Lounge Bar, things are quiet. The barman is polishing glasses. In the old dining-room to the left, which is now the Siren Suite for special functions, preparations are being completed for what looks like a drinks reception. At the end of the hall, where a sign says Dolphin Restaurant, I glance down steps and see tables laid but no one eating. No sign of Mary Ryan, the supervisor, whom I met one night in Joys.

—Where's your Bloomsday merriment? I ask the girl at the reception desk.

—In the Viennese Bar, she says, pointing towards a corridor off the left of the hall.

—Could we eat something hot? Preferably liver and bacon.

—I'm afraid we only have sandwiches now, she says. You can order them in the Viennese Bar.

—I am disappointed, I say, I thought you'd have the dinner that Bloom ate here. After all, he made your hotel famous.

I need a hot meal in the middle of the day, or even at this time. I hate eating sandwiches for lunch, or rather, my stomach hates it. The ritual gorgonzola sandwich in Davy Byrne's was more than enough for one day.

—So there you are, Miranda, I say, I'm sorry about that. We should have had the coddle.

She says she doesn't mind, that sandwiches will do her fine, so I don't tell her that I will hate them.

We go to the Viennese Bar which is a bright room with a bar near the door and people sitting at tables. Several of the Davy Byrne's crowd are here. Rosemary Wilton of course and her crew. Gerald Davis in his bowler, and Jim Carroll still doing Joyce. John Ryan, looking vacant and passive, is sitting with Christine Falls. Behind the bar, in flouncy dresses with bonnets, two girls are presumably Miss Kennedy and Miss Douce. But neither is really blonde, they are variations of brunette. With relief I take off my raincoat, fold it, and lay it on the floor beside a vacant chair at the table where John and Christine are sitting. We join them.

—How's it going, John? Weighed down by your labours?

—I just do what I'm told, says John who is still drinking burgundy. When they tell me to, I utter.

They have sandwiches, salad sandwiches, and tell us to help ourselves. Miranda does so happily. I do so *faute de mieux*. I like that, *faute de mieux*. Very much so, but I am hungry. A young man is reading aloud at the bar and the camera is focussed on him. I go there and ask the lighter brunette for a beer, and a Bacardi-and-coke for Miranda. Gerald Davis is leaning on the bar listening, but takes time off to whisper:

—I've an exhibition tonight in the Arts Club. Will you come?

—Thanks, Leopold. I'll see. But I think my itinerary will ordain otherwise. *You* should know about that.

Back at the table John says:

—I asked that one you were talking to which she was, Miss Kennedy or Miss Douce, and she said, I don't know anything about that. The manager just told us to put these clothes on.

I light my pipe and reach the lit match to Miranda's lips.

— Come on now, do your act. Eat that.

She opens her mouth, I insert the match, she draws her breath in and extinguishes it.

—Very good, very good. Nothing like keeping in practice.

—Is that your party trick? asks Christine.

—It's my job, says Miranda. Seriously.

And then who appears but Nina Witoszek.

—Hello, I say, where have *you* come from? Oslo, Oxford, Galway?

—From Galway, she says, today. Pat's with me but he's gone to do some research.

—I sent him something the other day, I say.

Then I introduce her all round, and she asks is anything happening.

—Well, there's us, I say. But apart from that, there just seems to be that guy reading at the bar.

He is not visible, being surrounded by a small circle of attentive people.

—But later, I gather, there's to be a reception in the Siren Suite out there. Our Lord Mayor, Carmencita, is coming and they're launching a poster of Joycean Dublin and so to speak unveiling that plaque on the wall outside.

—I'll go and listen, says Nina, throwing us a smile and a wave and joining the circle at the bar.

I have ordered a plate of beef sandwiches to get some substance at least, and the lighter brunette, Miss Kennedy we'll say, brings them.

—Come over here, says John to her, till I show you where you can read all about yourself.

He takes up the Book, flicks through it, and stops. She leans over his shoulder.

—Miss Kennedy was a blonde, and Miss Douce a brunette. Gold and bronze he called them.

Then, reading aloud:

—Am I awfully sunburnt?

Miss Bronze unbloused her neck.

—No, said Miss Kennedy. It gets brown after. Did you try the borax with the cherry laurel water?

Miss Douce halfstood to see her skin askance in the barmirror gildedlettered where hock and claret glasses shimmered and in their midst a shell.

—And leave it to my hands, she said.

—Try it with the glycerine, Miss Kennedy advised.

—That was here? says the girl, peering at the page. That's very interesting. We must read it. What page is it?

—From page 254 on, says John, in this Penguin edition. The chapter's called The Sirens, but you won't find that written over it.

She goes away, and Christine says:

—Your good deed for today.

John smiles seraphically. Miranda, who has been silent for a while, taking it all in, sees me looking at my watch.

—Have you got to go? she asks.

—Yes, I say, I have to meet a man at the Four Courts at twenty to five for the walk to Barney Kiernan's pub back of the markets.

—I'll stay here another few minutes, and then go. I've to be somewhere at five. Thanks a million, it's been very interesting. Wasn't I lucky to bump into you? And thanks again for the book.

—You were very patient, I say, as I stand up and put on my coat.

We exchange kisses.

—Maybe you'd like to wander into the reception before you go. I'll ring you before you leave for France. Bye John, bye Christine, must be on my way.

At the bar the reading is over, but Nina is still standing there. I have been thinking that with Jim Gorry not feeling so well, I mightn't have company for the nighttown part. So I take out my DART timetable and struggle with the rows of figures. To travel to Killester and get a train back to Connolly, the latest I can take from Westland Row is at 11.02. On my way out I stop beside Nina.

—Would you ever tell Pat I'd love him to join me for a Bloomsday adventure tonight. At the DART station on Westland Row at eleven. Better, five to eleven. There might be another friend along. We'd be doing nighttown.

She says she'll tell him that. Through the door of the Siren Suite I see Carmencita beaming amid a score or so of people with glasses in their hands. I leave my *Irish Independent* on a chair in the hall.

Turning right along the quay in the direction of the Four Courts, I stop at the corner of Arran Street and look intently into the window of Gifts Exchange, Surplus Gifts Bought and Sold. There is a Hi-Fi (recording not working) £80. A Right Angle beard and moustache trimmer costs £12.50, and a bicycle mirror £1.50. The sandwiches are leaden in my stomach. The traffic roaring past makes discretion unnecessary. I try hard, manage it, and continue.

4.30 - 6.15

ORMOND QUAY VIA CULHANE'S
TO SANDYMOUNT

The sun's heat has gathered through the day and the great, blazing star is still adding to it. Across the river, beyond the Civic Offices, on a height at some remove, Christ Church is coming into view: first the Synod building and the archway over Winetavern Street connecting it with the cathedral; then gradually the cathedral itself. Suddenly I become aware that a boy of about eighteen, walking towards me along the quay wall, has taken a red and white life-belt off the spike it was hanging on and thrown it into the river. Dodging two cars I cross to intercept him. His hair is close-cut and he is wearing a green jumper and blue jeans.

—Why did you do that? I ask him, looking at the life-belt floating down the middle of the river. Don't you know people have drowned because there was no life-belt to save them?

—It fucking fell off, didn't you see it? he says, and continues walking towards Capel Street Bridge.

I feel angry and frustrated. Looking up and down the quay, I can see no guard. Telephoning them would mean going back to the Ormond, and I am to meet Paddy McEntee at twenty to five. Returning to the footpath, I find myself at a railinged area just before West Charles Street joins the quay. Five cars are parked in it beside lofty wooden buttresses that are propping up the wall of No. 34. It is a post-office with

the offices of James O'Connor, solicitor, in the storeys above
it. Converting, mentally, two shillings and sixpence into
decimal coinage, I enter the post-office and ask the man for
a postal order for twelve and a half pence.

—Fifty pence is the smallest we do, he says.

—Well then could I have one for two pounds and six
pence?

—I'll give you one for two pounds and put a sixpenny
stamp on it.

He does that, and I pay him the money. You never know,
it might come in useful. Leaving, I see ahead of me the great
pile of the Four Courts, Gandon's second masterpiece, front-
ing the next quay. People call it "Gandon's second masterpiece", but Gandon only executed it: Thomas Cooley
designed it. To enter it I must turn into Chancery Place. As I
reach the corner, I see a guard standing at the opposite corner,
cross over to him, and wait while he advises and consoles a
young American man whose bicycle has been stolen. Reflecting that the thrower-away of life-belts will be beyond Capel
Street Bridge by now—but in which direction?—I note that
the garda is carrying a walkie-talkie. Except for the traffic
lights, one-way signs and lamp-posts intervening, I have a
full view of Gothic Christ Church such as one could not
have before the clearance was made for the Civic Offices.
The Vikings had a church there before the Normans built
this one. I was in the crypt and saw Strongbow's tomb. A
grass lawn slopes down from it to trees along the quay and a
long Esso tanker waiting at the lights. The traffic appears at
speed in the archway and is poured through it down to the
bridge and across into Chancery Place. It was at the next
bridge upriver, or thereabouts, that the ford strewn with
hurdles, the *Áth Cliath*, crossed the river. There the ancient
road *Slige Mhidhluachra* from the North joined the road from
Tara and crossed to meet the *Slige Mhór* from the West.
Hurdlefordtown was at that junction. As the sea-going town

downriver extended to embrace it, the names *Dubhlinn* and *Baile Átha Cliath,* both Gaelic, both laid claim to the amalgam stubbornly. When the inlanders learned to speak a smattering of English, they doubtless had to say "Dublin", but when they used their own language, they stuck to *their* name—even when a bridge had replaced the ford, and when centuries later their language had ceased to be spoken there and was used as a vernacular only on the far-off Atlantic coast. So it is that name now, *Baile Átha Cliath,* which franks the 560,000 letters and parcels postmarked in Dublin every day. The pubs hereabouts have legal names. The Chancery Inn which I just passed, the black Tilted Wig over there in Chancery Place. The American goes off unhappy and I perform my citizen's duty.

—People have drowned, you know, for lack of a life-belt, I conclude.

—Thanks, says the garda.

He fingers his radio, crosses back the way I have come, and is stopped by someone as he reaches the other corner.

I quicken my steps into Chancery Place. Legal-looking men carrying thin briefcases, bulging ones, or piles of files, pass to and from the Four Courts gate. I cross the yard and enter the hall of the Bar Library. To either side of the pale yellow, light-reflecting floor, groups of people sit at long tables, most of them silent and with an air of expectancy as in a dentist's waiting-room. Catherine McGuinness and another barrister, a man, both in gowns, are talking with two of the groups. Reaching the hatch of the Library, I stand while the dark-uniformed man inside it listens to a woman beside me and calls "Roger Sweetman" into a microphone. Behind him, on long desks, papers and books are piled. The walls are shelves of worn, well-bound books. A barrister is up a ladder taking out a book. Others are sitting, standing, talking into phones. The clock shows nearly a quarter to five. Seamus Sorahan, senior gentleman of the Bar in gown and wig, files under his arm, approaches the crier, murmurs something to him with serious mien, and leaves through the doorway to my right.

—Patrick McEntee is expecting me, I say.

—He was consulting until a minute ago, says the crier, pointing to a door off the hall. I saw him come out.

He grasps his microphone and calls "Patrick McEntee". I pace back through the hall. The Civil War began in this building, shells falling into it from Government guns across the river. Through a window I see into the courtyard, and the Public Records Office beyond it where the archives of centuries were burnt. As I turn back towards the hatch, Paddy McEntee comes towards me, papers under his arm.

—I'm ready, he says. Let's go.

—Are you in the McGimpsey case? I ask him, as we make for the door.

—No, I'm in an armed robbery case in the Circuit Criminal Court. I've been defending a man called Alford.

—The McGimpsey case is being heard here, isn't it?

Paddy says yes, it's in the High Court. We pass out into the sun.

—Don't mind the raincoat, I say. I took it because the morning was dull, and got stuck with it.

—I was thinking, he says, that this is the perfect Bloomsday. The sixteenth of June and the Thursday of the Ascot Gold Cup. I belong to that sect which regards the Thursday of the Ascot Gold Cup as the real Bloomsday, and as you know that isn't always on June sixteenth.

—It's also the year of the Dublin Millennium, for whatever that's worth.

At the gate we turn left and soon are facing the ugly block of the Motor Taxation building on Chancery Street. I move towards the corner of Greek Street.

—What are you going that way for? asks Paddy. There's nothing there, only Corporation flats. He'd have gone right through the markets.

—Well, in the Ormond he said to himself he'd "dodge round by Greek Street", and you come to the markets that way too.

—He changed his mind. Wasn't he seen "sloping around" here "counting up all the guts of the fish"? He'd have to go through St Michan's Street, that's where he'd see the fish. And all those vegetables and fruit and other squelchy things. That's what he'd head for.

I am persuaded, so we turn right along Chancery Street past Hughes's pub where they have good Irish music, and Fegan's Catering Supplies and Cash and Carry, and turn left into St Michan's Street.

—I think you're right, I say. He is described as approaching Barney Kiernan's "through Michan's land".

Of course, all of this area is probably in the parish of St Michan's old church where as a boy I shook hands with the Crusader's mummy in the crypt, but the street of that name and its immediate surroundings would seem to fit the bill most specifically. Fifty paces into the street the markets begin, and occupy the rest of both sides. On the left the fish-market, on the right fruit and vegetables. The fish-market is plain red-brick with square, unadorned entrances. A warehouse in Ostia, I think; utilitarian Roman. And in the same vein, looking at the opposite side, I think of the municipal market in Antioch, say, under the Empire; Hellenistic baroque. There is a succession of blind arches, topped with yellow brick, along the red-brick wall. Several arched openings, a magnificent main entrance, and decorative iron-work in round windows. The market-day is ending. They have been here since very early, hours before I set out from Eccles Street. Wooden crates, plastic bags and paper are strewn around. A bent old man is sorting through wooden trays of discarded tomatoes and peaches, and placing his booty in two plastic bags.

—Look at those tiles there, aren't they beautiful? says Paddy.

The red tiles he is pointing to are above the line of arches. They have three-dimensional patterns of leaves surrounding a central blossom. Through a doorway we see the many-coloured fruits of the earth displayed in box after box in a stall that seems to be still open for casual trading. An Indian and his Irish wife are looking at melons, a small boy answering them. The fish-market, inside, is a great empty hall with iron pillars, traders' names suspended over sections. A man is playing a hose on the floor. On the footpath at our feet lies a fish head. We stop at the principal entrance of the fruit-market, which is flanked on each side by two Corinthian pillars supporting an elaborate entablature with a long inscription saying that it was opened in 1892. In the tympanum of the arch, the Dublin coat of arms. Paddy, gazing up at a relief sculpture which tops it all, says:

—Look at the swift and the butterfly. Isn't that lovely?

At first I cannot see the butterfly. Then I do, with delight; it is so delicately done. It is to the left of the swift, hovering with it over a horizontal, drooping chain of fruit and vegetables. To be even, I say:

—And you see the seagull?

He scans the picture, furrows his brow, then looks higher and sees it, a live one, perched on top of it all. Several young buddleias are growing from various parts of the entablature, and looking back along the roof of the market I see more. Suddenly the plant's other name, the Butterfly Tree, seems appropriate, and the fate of that butterfly trapped in stone Tantalean.

—Do you come through here often? I ask Paddy. Sometimes, he says, when I'm going to Green Street.

—That's where the Special Criminal Court is?

—Yes, he says, and sometimes the Circuit Court if the Four Courts are too crowded.

At the corner where the street joins Mary's Lane, a woman is picking some usable red peppers out of a discarded crate of them. Two entrances to the fruit-market give onto Mary's Lane. Along this street—it is by no means a lane—and in the side-streets off it, are the warehouses of the fruit and vegetable merchants. Some of them are closed. Half an hour earlier and we'd have seen a busy traffic of forklifts moving to and fro between the market and the warehouses. Now only two are making their last trips. The air is laden with fruit fragrance.

Walking to the left a few paces along Mary's Lane we come to the car-park at the side of the fish-market. In big white letters on the red wall someone has written "Prison is where big criminals send little criminals".

—I hope you take that to heart, I say.

—Why me? says Paddy. Sure I spend most of my time trying to keep them out of it.

Then we turn back, and see "Rhonda F is cool" scribbled on the closed gate of Fruit Importers Ireland.

—Besides, says Paddy, there are the Rhondas. That is surely a mitigating factor. Do you know, by the way, that those people, FII Fyffes, have made Ireland into Europe's banana emporium? They got the courts to recognise banana ripening as a manufacturing process, thereby benefiting by the special low tax rate for manufacturers. So the world's bananas are shipped here to be ripened, and then on to Europe. We are really and truly, in the most literal sense, the banana republic. Joyce would have liked that.

Brendan's Coffee Shop is closed. At the corner of Halston Street, above Potato Sales, the Federation of Irish Cyclists have their sign.

—Joyce would have liked that too, says Paddy, reading it aloud.

Flowers, of course, they sell flowers here also. A discarded pile of them is lying outside the other main entrance to the fruit-market. Above it, flanking the city's coat of arms, two female figures, one of them holding green scales which are swaying in an air current. A fruit fragrance hovers outside Doran's, but it is strongest at the First National Fruit Company where there are still piles of boxes and crates: Irish tomatoes, Uruguayan mandarins, oranges from Morocco and Cyprus, melons from Spain, and iceberg lettuces. On the corner where Arran Street meets Mary's Lane we face a large three-storey house in Andalusian style: stippled white plaster, windows with black wrought-iron grilles, faded geraniums in pots on the window-sills. The Smithwicks beer-sign suggests a pub but it seems closed.

—Is it a pub and if so why is it closed? I ask.

—Probably it opened in the early morning, Paddy says, as the pubs around here do. Probably it will open again tonight. This is siesta time.

The markets, like the docks, have special licences.

We turn left into Little Green Street and, walking on the shaded side, notice the cool. As it happens, North Pole Company and McNulty's Arctic Refrigeration are here, but I decide that it's the shade is making us cool. A street of colours. The green and dun brown of Keeling's big warehouse and loading bay; red and white of McNulty's; blue and yellow of Carton's Manor Farm Chickens vans shunting in a shed running through to Halston Street; the brutal dun, white and yellow garishness of the Molly Malones pub. A fine view back down the street and through Arran Street to the Civic Offices across the river. At the far end we emerge in what looks like a little square in a sleepy Spanish provincial town. Plane trees, a low wall and railings around a small, raised park; two old men sitting on one of the benches, and children playing. Little Britain Street runs to the left and right. Straight ahead is Green Street with the courthouse on the left beyond the park, and Culhane's small pub almost directly across from it. Helped by the trees, sun and shadow are beautifully mingled, and it is quiet except for the children's cries and the hum of traffic from Capel Street.

—Barney Kiernan's was in Numbers 8 and 9 there, says Paddy, pointing to two houses standing between waste spaces on the right-hand arm of Little Britain Street. A daughter of the man who owns Culhane's, Pat O'Keeffe, has the hairdressing salon in No. 8.

As You Like It, says the green and yellow sign, Ladies' Salon, Unisex Salon Downstairs.

—What's the statue in the park?

I see a female figure on a pedestal.

—It's to commemorate Newgate Prison, says Paddy. She's the Maid of Erin. The prison used stand there.

We walk a bit up Green Street and enter the park. I see that the woman is wearing an embroidered cloak and bears a wreath in her hand. There is a wolfhound beside her and the top of a Celtic cross shows behind her. All the patriotic paraphernalia of the 1880s, say. The inscription in Irish on the front is very worn and difficult to decipher. Behind, in English, it is somewhat clearer, but the black paint has gone off some of the letters, leaving them a ghostly white. "Within this park once stood Newgate Prison associated in dark and evil days with the doing to death of Confessors of Irish liberty who gave their lives to vindicate their country's right to national independence. This memorial is erected to perpetuate their memory . . . to honour their motives and to inculcate a grateful"—something—"in Irish minds." Something at the end about "regenerating our fatherland from subjection." And "W.K. is cool". At the back of the park, towards the courthouse, there are two handball alleys, and on the wall of one of them, in white, "Provos *Tiocfaidh Ár Lá*." Our Day Will Come. That's what some IRA men shout in court when they are being led off to prison. Probably they have shouted it in the courthouse next door where the Special Criminal Court without jury has been set up to try them. But they are no longer "done to death", and instead of Newgate they are sent to Portlaoise. We have left the park, passed metal crowd-barriers standing ready for protests, and are looking at the rear of the courthouse—Paddy tells me it's the rear. The pillars set into the wall give it a sort of dignity, but nothing else does. The facade is blotched here and there by new granite blocks of a different colour than the old ones. The lower windows have iron bars and there is a rectangle of yellowish paint on the wall with AN CHÚIRT written on it and a hand pointing. Paddy says it closed at four. They were hearing a case about some fellows up in Monaghan, his own county, who overturned a police car during the funeral for an IRA man who had been shot by the SAS.

—It was here, wasn't it, I say, that many of the *Speeches from the Dock* were made?

That was the collection of patriots' "speeches before sentence" which used to be, so to speak, in every Irish household.

—Oh yes indeed, says Paddy, it's there for nearly two hundred years. It was opened in 1797, just in time to deal with the rebellion.

Except for the crude concrete factory building adjoining it—we see girls at machines through windows—Culhane's has jungle lots to left and right. On our way into the bar we pass a snug and I think: that's where people from the courthouse gather in huddles during sessions. The television is on. It sounds like a comedy programme, for it emits occasional collective laughs. A few men, two of them reading tabloids, are seated on stools at the bar. In the backroom, which I can see into, pool is being played. There are two men at one of the small tables by the wall. We sit at the next table, which bears a Bulmer's ashtray and Carlsberg Lager beer pads. Paddy wants a coffee because he still has work to do at home. Ordering it and a beer for myself at the counter, I hear one of the men on the stools say "Great to see a copper gettin it all the same". He looks like an old sailor with his heavy stubble and long coarse pullover. Behind the counter, between the Malibu bottle and packages of Gillette razors, a card is pinned up, headed Culhane's Overseas Club Nap Results, and there are figures written on it. Some light is coming from the open door, but most of it is from the two fluorescent bars above the counter. It is mercifully cool, so I leave my coat on, open. The sounds from the TV are by far the loudest in the bar, except for cries occasionally from the pool-players. "Good shot!" "That's easy now." "Take the shot again". Or, in parody of the notice about smoking on the wall, "No singing over pool-table!" There is desultory talk, inaudible to us who are a few feet away, between the men at the bar and between them and Tony, the barman. Occasionally, shouts, competing with the TV, cross the room in various directions. Paddy has been calling in here for thirty years. He wants me to meet the owner, Pat O'Keeffe, and Tony says he'll be out shortly. Paddy nods towards the mottled glass partition around the snug.

—He used have a cat that would sit on top of that all day farting at the hams.

There are two hams hanging from the partition inside the counter, and Paddy tells me they are raffled every Friday. Pat O'Keeffe comes over slowly and sits down with us. Paddy doesn't bother introducing me, which I like. He brings the conversation around to history.

—I came here in 1952, says Pat. I bought the houses around the corner, from where Anne has the hairdressing salon to here, but they were in such a state that the Corporation said they had to be demolished. I put up the factory next door to give support to this house, so that it wouldn't have to come down too. But I re-built this house from the ground floor up. It must have been three hundred years old.

There is a quiz on the TV now and the men at the counter are attending to it, trying to answer the questions. A woman in a tweed jacket comes in, gets cigarettes and an orange drink at the bar, and sits down beside a man at the table on the other side of us.

—Was there any trace of a pub there, I ask, when you bought No. 8 on Little Britain Street?

—Not a trace, says Pat. That was long before. But the house next door, No. 9, looks as if it might have been part of a pub once.

The sailor man has turned around from the counter and is calling, "Sparkie, Sparkie, come here, Sparkie", to a tawny cat that has appeared on the floor, stretching itself. A man in a leather jacket comes in carrying four or five picture-frames of different sizes which he leaves down at the counter. A young fellow beside him takes one up and looks through it at one of the men at the table beside us.

—Hey Jim, how do you like to see me framed?

—Who are your customers? I ask Pat.

—Lorry-drivers, chaps from the markets, and the locals.

Nodding towards a man drinking quietly at the bar, he adds:

—That's Brendan there who has the coffee-shop. Did you see the old prints in the back?

Shyly, because I am aware that my strange presence has been quietly noticed, I go into the pool-room. There is an engraving of "The State Trial of Daniel O'Connell 1843". Rows of seated men in knee-breeches, the Liberator in the dock. Moving along the wall, I come to a framed group of five photographs of revolutionary leaders, with de Valera in the central position. Collins and Griffith are there. The other old print is on the next wall, "The United Irish Patriots of 1798", a collection of portraits. One of the pool-players has just pocketed the black.

—Well done, John, says the loser.

—Ah, says the winner, sure God is good and the divil can't be that bad.

—You're right there, you know, I say as I pass him.

The woman in the tweed coat is leaving.

—See ya, Tom. See ya, Tony.

—They're lovely, I tell Pat. They must be very old.

—They were in the house when I came here and long before that, he says.

Yes, when this was a place where working men talked politics and political trials, all the big issues of the day, and those prints reflected their shared interests. Two men come in, one of them carrying a bunch of keys.

—Ah here's the O'Rourkes, says the sailor man. Drinks on all the house. I see yer pocket bulgin with the winnins.

The two men sit down at the wall, smiling.

—Hey Tony, two pints there, says the one with the keys.

—If y'were any good now, y'd buy me a pint, the sailor man persists.

—I gave you some blocks you never paid me for, says O'Rourke.

—Go on, buy me a pint.

—If you give me back the blocks.

There are ads on the TV and my watch says it's getting on for a quarter to six. I tell Paddy I had better call a taxi. He says to ask Tony, he'll get me one. So I go to the counter and ask Tony to phone the nearest rank.

—We always use VIP, he says. They give good service.

I say "to Sandymount" and he goes to the phone and after a few seconds says, "Culhane's. Gentleman going to Sandymount".

The RTE News begins on the television. Mrs Thatcher has been talking about the "terrible atrocity in Lisburn".

—I'll be going now, says Pat. Nice meeting you.

—I'll be seeing you, he says to Paddy.

He moves away slowly. The next meeting of the Anglo-Irish Conference will have security at the top of its agenda. The McGimpsey case continued today at the High Court. The Belfast brothers, Michael and Christopher McGimpsey, both members of the Official Unionist Party, are challenging the Anglo-Irish Agreement on the grounds that it conflicts with the Constitution of the Republic, and particularly with Article 2 which says that the national territory embraces the whole island. They argue that the Intergovernmental Conference established by the Agreement involves an acceptance by the Government of the sovereignty of the United Kingdom over Northern Ireland, and also that they, personally, being Ulster unionists, had been treated as aliens or non-Irish inasmuch as they had not been consulted in the negotiation of the Agreement. Today Counsel for the State has been answering these arguments. The Agreement did not mean that either government had conceded any diminution of its territorial sovereignty. Moreover, there was no obligation on either government to consult any particular group of its citizens. They were empowered to negotiate on behalf of all the citizens of their respective states.

—The McGimpseys have a sense of humour, I say to Paddy. Do you think they've a chance?

—Not a snowball's in hell.

The younger of the two men who have been sitting at the table next to us gets up to leave.

—See yiz tomorrow night, he says, glancing around him.

A taximan appears in the doorway and I stand up and signal to him.

—I'll be with you now.

It took ten minutes to come. Paddy stands up too.

—I'd better get home, he says.

His car is at the Four Courts. I say I'll give him a lift, but he prefers to walk.

—Well, Paddy, I say, thanks a million. It was a real pleasure. You've been a great help to me.

—Oh I'm glad to have marked the day, he says, even in a little way.

I thank Tony and we both leave.

—Sorry for the delay, says the driver as he opens the rear door for me to enter. This time of the evening it's hard to move. What part of Sandymount?

—The Green, I tell him.

We drive to Capel Street which is chock-a-block with cars, vans and buses waiting to cross the river or turn left along the quays. The rush hour has passed its peak but is not over yet. Here a man, there a girl, pulls down a shutter or turns a key in a shop door. Gerald Davis's gallery is already shuttered. Left now along the quays and the traffic is still slow-moving. The tall green crane in the Custom House Quay Project is motionless again. Lady Commerce on the Custom House dome gleams white in the western sun and Liberty Hall could not be whiter. Carpet City on a van ahead. As good a name for it as any. Car pet city. "No car should be without its pet. We have a wide choice ranging from bunny rabbits to harmless snakes." Right now across O'Connell Bridge.

—It isn't ideal, says the taximan. I'd normally go across the new bridge, the one below Butt Bridge, but the traffic gave me the opportunity.

Queues for buses in Westmoreland Street. Left along Townsend street, the gasometer far ahead of us, buses hemming us in. A DART train crossing the railway bridge transects the gasometer. After Tara Street and a glimpse of the Poolbeg chimneys, the traffic eases and we are quickly past Lombard Street and the Pearse House flats, and by Lower Sandwith Street have reached Pearse Street and the main road to our destination. The still water of the Grand Canal Basin at Boland's Mill. Over the hump-backed bridge and through Ringsend into Irishtown, all the houses mellowed by the sunlight. Newbridge Avenue passes to the right, and that must be the Star of the Sea, a neo-gothic aisled church built of unshaped granite. By tree-lined Sandymount Road we reach the heart of Sandymount around the Green.

—Just anywhere here, I say.

He leaves me by the high wall of a castellated, ochre-coloured house with pointed windows. The fare is £3.90 plus £1.15 pick-up charge, but he makes that £1.10, so it is five pounds straight. The journey took sixteen minutes.

I walk to Gloria and Louis Pieterse's house. They are expecting me for dinner.

SANDYMOUNT STRAND VIA HOLLES STREET TO MERRION HALL

It is twenty past eight and Louis and Gloria have gone to Gerald Davis's exhibition in the Arts Club. Walking from their house I reach Strand Road by Seafort Avenue. At last, across strand and water, I am looking directly at the Poolbeg chimneys, less than a mile away, and between them I glimpse a bit of Howth Head across the bay. To the southeast Dún Laoghaire harbour juts out, and Dalkey rising to Killiney closes the bay. The strand, bare of its shallow water, stretches towards the stone and grass of the South Wall where the red-and-white banded chimneys rise. To the left of them, towards the city, the red bulk of the disused Ringsend power station. Beside me, along the road which skirts the strand, a line of cars are parked. Girls and women in shorts and singlets are walking in twos and threes or alone. On their backs I read Premier Milk Dairies Bloomsday Run. One of them tells me it took place at half-seven on the beach.

As I turn left along Strand Road it becomes Beach Road, an outdated name because the beach ends now and is replaced by a wide stretch of filled-in, grassy parkland extending towards the Ringsend power station and, on the city side of it, the Irish Glass factory. Beyond the factory, towards the Liffey mouth, I see cranes and other harbour

paraphernalia reduced by the distance. Beach Road itself is on land reclaimed from the strand this century. Short streets join it from the left. One of them will be Leahy's Terrace. Some men pass in singlets and shorts, but very few. It's the women who have really taken to this running business. Partly for slimming, I suppose, or to keep slim, but I think they also like the feeling of running around the streets in what amounts to underwear. I am struck by their thighs which, as one would expect, are taut and good to look at. Near the junction with Marine Drive there's a small marquee, two caravans, and a big band of Premier Fresh Milk people. Children and teenagers are standing or running, some of them drinking the milk which the Premier Milk people are dispensing free. On the low wall between footpath and park, in their white uniforms with black lettering, a group of happy boys and girls of the Dublin Sandwich Board Company are seated.

—Were you the people who were doing Bewley's today?

—Yes, say three of them, laughing.

—You remember me? asks one of the girls.

—Of course, I say, how could I forget you?

I cross a stile into the park and here's this great big pointed Cliodna Cussen stone set up in a sandy space among shrubs. She seems to be really into pillar-stones. In front of it a notice, An Gallán Gréine, which means the Sun Pillar. *Do James Joyce* in red paint on a stone at its base—not do him of course, but "to" him in another language. A man's voice through a loudspeaker, asking Finbar O'Driscoll to please come to the commentary position, flashes me an image of a wandering child. Cliodna has told me that this pillar-stone is aligned with another stone which points towards the sunset at the winter solstice. Looking around, I see a smaller pointed stone some distance away, in the direction of that multi-coloured, much-admired Ringsend housing-estate, another example of the new-style Corporation housing. Like an explorer in deepest somewhere I set off across the grass to investigate. The cries of the children recede. Over towards the Irish Glass factory, boys are playing soccer. I pass more people in twos and threes walking and drinking milk. I am taken by the great sense of holiday and fun and of people really enjoying themselves on this balmy sunny evening. Heaven, I suppose, is something like this, nothing spectacular, just being. And it happens occasionally on earth. Now I'm beside the smaller pointed stone, looking back towards the big one, which means I'm looking roughly towards Dalkey, and I cannot imagine what Dalkey has to do with sunset at the winter solstice or any other time. So I don't really know what all of this is about. Maybe it's sunrise. Turning my back to the bigger stone and looking at this one, I see a lot of straight lines on it and they seem to be pointing towards the east. I must clear this up with Cliodna. But what use is the alignment, or whatever it is, if no one knows it's there?

I return to the road and continue towards Ringsend, watching out for Leahy's Terrace which should join the road soon. Cars and cyclists are cruising past me. Looking back I see the Premier Milk caravans almost in the distance now. Here's Leahy's Terrace, and up the street the Star of the Sea church. Five to nine. An hour to go to sunset. I suppose you could call it twilight. I was going to take a picture here, hoping for a view of Howth and the Baily lighthouse. But what do I see? Lines of young trees in the park and the big factory in the background.

As I walk up Leahy's Terrace, a woman in a car parked on its own is showing an ABC picture book to a small child. What made her sit here by herself away from the revels? It was here near the house called Cosy Lodge that the beach used begin. The Star of the Sea stands in grounds with bushes and trees around the perimeter, but there is direct access to the front across some paving. Closed, unfortunately. I'd have had to come earlier to see inside. "Pregnant and worried?" A picture of a girl's face. "Cura cares. You have a friend to help you in confidence." Phone some number. "Before you get married get ready. To book your pre-marriage course in the Dublin area ring . . ." A picture of a couple together on their knees. "The Hanly Centre, Dún Laoghaire. A counselling and information service for those whose lives have been affected by a drinking problem. Help is available." All of that is good to know. I leave the church grounds and walk towards Newbridge Avenue. On Northumberland Road I will get a bus to Holles Street. Here is the ecclesiastical-looking building which this morning, for a moment, I thought might be the Star of the Sea. I ask a man passing with his dog what it is. It used to be a Presbyterian church, but that closed, he says, about ten years ago.

—It's used as a church hall by the Presbyterians and Church of Ireland people. RTE uses it now and again.

Do I remember, or am I mistaken, that Jack White trained me and other would-be television interviewers there about a year before television began? But that was more than ten years ago.

On Newbridge Avenue I am the only pedestrian. This morning's scene with the jaunting-cars and the happy people seems like a dream. The houses have a weathered look and gentle gardens. As I cross the Dodder I now have a back view of the towering East Stand of the rugby stadium. The rows of concrete pillars, forming right-angles like L's upside down—or like the hammers inside a piano—underpin that aerial leap of the stand which I admired earlier. And they too look very good. Physically uplifting, they also do that to the heart. Past the stadium's numbered gates and over the level crossing, and I am in the luxurious part of Lansdowne Road. Grand red-brick houses and old chestnut trees. The Institute of Public Administration has several of them. Tom Barrington was director there for years. What I know about decentralisation and the "service" approach to government—government as humanism—I learned from his writings. We have just been through two years of the Constitution Club together. At dinner Louis showed me Tom's book on Kerry, where he has a cottage and spends much of his time, and I said that was the other side of Tom, his secret love-life, so to speak. The houses are regal now, with high steps up. A mellowed, well-worn part of suburban Dublin.

Crossing Shelbourne Road, I enter the final stretch. Hugh and Helga Staunton in No. 30. I thought of Hugh this morning at the Mater; he works there, and I hoped I might run into him in Davy Byrne's to talk about it. The grandiose Berkeley Court Hotel, its name another instance of the vogue for English names. Charlie Haughey used go to lunch there. I lunched there with him and Seán Feehan, the publisher, playing matchmaker to their brief love affair. It began with Seán's books about yachting off the Cork and Kerry coasts, but soon for Seán it was political too, and he wrote that book about Charlie the Statesman which he has now bitterly retracted with his *Apology to the Irish People*. The rank of taxis snakes around the corner onto Pembroke Road becoming Merrion Road on the way from the city to Dún Laoghaire and beyond. Jury's International Hotel, the all-purpose night and day hostelry, its foyer like a busy airport lounge; last recourse of late-night eaters and the place where all-night parties go for breakfast; stopover for bussed Americans on their European or world tours. Once, after we had been working at something into the night, Jim Fitzgerald, the theatre man, took three of us there by taxi in the hope of getting a drink before closing-time; but no go, we were late. Jim stood then in the plaza among the cars, and looking up at the rows of lamps lit in bedrooms, storey upon storey, stamped his foot and called out:

—Hey! You! Americans! This is *not* Istanbul, this is Dublin.

Protest and revenge. I remember Jury's when it was on Dame Street not far from the vanished Moira; its beautiful old wooden bar which is now in some *Gasthof* in Zürich. From the 60s on, the office-blocks have crept out here to rendezvous with the new hotels and expensive restaurants in this salubrious social climate. Lansdowne House and the octagonal building of Allied Irish Banks. If not quite an extension of the central city area, then an annexe to it.

I cross Lansdowne Road to the other corner, and then Northumberland Road to a bus stop. A 45 arrives and for 45p takes me in less than five minutes to Merrion Square, leaving me almost opposite Holles Street. The hospital, though called popularly by the street's name and having its main entrance on Holles Street, fronts formally onto the square, where the east and north sides meet. Standing on the corner near the park railing, I read "The National Maternity Hospital" and that it was founded in 1894. But the present building is from the 1930s. Probably the main entrance would be here but for the fact that the landlord, the Countess of Pembroke, stipulated in the lease that no entrance for people attending the hospital would be on the square. So they made this part the nurses' home.

It is nine-thirty and I am not due at the hospital until a quarter to ten. Thursday is late opening night for the National Gallery, but it closed at nine. Verna and David James have just passed me driving. They stopped a second, and since they are regulars at the Arts Club, I asked them were they going to the exhibition, and they were. I might have taken a lift, but there would have been time only to put my head in and walk back. I told you, Gerry, my itinerary ordains otherwise. I will stroll in the park. So I follow the railings up the east side to the gate.

It is a lovely evening after a splendid day. From a reddish grey sky the sunlight is falling on the fronts of the Georgian houses making them rose-pink. Ahead, at the end of a long perspective, there is a view to the blue mountains. I enter the park through a tunnel of shrubs and come on six birch trees standing behind a bed of African marigolds not yet in bloom. Then the path divides and in the V is a bed of luscious geraniums with white and purple petunias, and pansies at the edges, yellow, blue and puce. Behind this, begonias are blooming in six small circles around trees. That grassy mound over there covers the ruins of a World War Two air-raid shelter. The sword converted to the plough-share, in a sense. Some days a band plays in front of it. I see a statue of a dejected woman over to the right and, walking across the grass to it, find that she is a full-bodied, bronze woman wearing what goes for Celtic dress, and leaning her head sadly on her right hand, while her left shoulder and arm rest on a harp without strings. The statue is backed by an upright granite slab on which I read, without surprise, that she is Éire, and that she was made by Jerome Connor 1876-1943. She was presented by Joseph Downes and Son, in 1976, "to commemorate the centenary of Buttercrust Bakery, Dublin and honour its founder, Sir Joseph Downes JP, High Sheriff of Dublin, and also to record its appreciation for the support of many generations of Dubliners, and for the enjoyment of the citizens of this city and all passers-by." There are great plane trees near the railings opposite Holles Street. It's in here of course that you can best see the splendour of the Square, just as you can see Nassau Street at its best from the park of Trinity. Back on the path I come on Busy Lizzies, red and purple, under maples. Then the big central lawn opens out. The gardeners have celebrated this grassy expanse with a floral archipelago: three large circles, four smaller ones, and four rectangles. What a lovely park this is! I think of Janet Wilson from New Zealand who lived near here during her year in Dublin. She took so much pleasure in these flowers. The tulips in May were her favourites; now it is time for the half-hardy annuals. Leaving the path, I move through the archipelago. Geraniums again, with purple petunias, edged with French marigolds. Masses of red salvia and white lobelia interspersed with light grey senecio. French marigolds mixed with Red Cloud petunias and bordered with blue flowers. Here a bed of white, pink and red begonias with red foliage is juxtaposed with a bed of green-leaved begonias. Redskin dahlias form the central circle, and near it a flaming array of Busy Lizzies surrounds a conifer. Where I regain the path there are white and pink carnations under a rhododendron after bloom. I have come now to the lawns at the end, opposite the National Gallery and Leinster House, where the bust of AE is almost hidden by untamed shrubs. This is a quiet part, undisturbed by the bugle calls of massed flowers. On the left there, among the trees towards the railing, Japan is remembered all the year round by a line of cherry trees, but more especially by one cherry planted by the Campaign for Nuclear Disarmament. In August, chrysanthemums are set under it for a ceremony in memory of Hiroshima.

I turn back towards the entrance. In one of those houses on the right is the Arts Council where I worked once for three months, and trod on important people's toes. The Director, Father O'Sullivan SJ, was a close friend of the important people, and he wrote me a letter from the Jesuit house of Mungret asking me to resign. I hated him for it, but in reaction I became an art critic and enjoyed that very much. Shrubs in tubs which I hadn't noticed. What love and imagination and expertise have been showered on this beautiful park. How fortunate for the men and women who work here, and plan and lay out and maintain all of this! This great space given to them to realise their floral and spatial dreams.

I reach the hospital entrance at a quarter to ten. The group of Georgian houses which formed the original hospital reached from the corner down Holles Street almost to this point. I tell the two young porters at the desk that I have arranged with the Administrator to see the rooms where the students and young doctors relax. They look at each other and say they have heard nothing of it, but one goes off to enquire and I sit down on a chair to wait. After a couple of minutes Jim Gorry puts his head in the door.

—There's the man himself, I cry, glad to see him, and rising to greet him.

He has Thérèse with him, he says, sitting in the car. Both of them come in, and the head porter emerges to say yes, he is to show me the rooms where the students and doctors relax and have their parties.

—It's just inside the door there, he says, in the part we call the Doctors' Res.

So the four of us go through the door and along a stretch of corridor, and the porter shows us a long room, simply furnished with a table, some chairs and a TV set. At one end of it is a table for table-tennis.

—That's the students' room, he says.

A few steps from it along the corridor, he shows us the doctors' room, and points through an open door at the end of it.

—That's the kitchen. They keep the beer there.

—Well, there you are, I say, we've seen what there is, and it gives one some idea. Thanks very much.

As we leave, Jim says he is still feeling a bit under the weather and won't stay late, but just for a drink. I hope Pat Sheeran got word from Nina and will turn up at Westland Row. We walk to the car.

—There used to be a pub, I say, called Burke's, around the bottom of this street, but I don't think it exists any more.

—It doesn't, says Jim. I should know the pubs around here. In my Sinn Féin days I used to sell *An Phoblacht* in all of them. I think Burke's used to be at the bottom on the left-hand side where there's a newspaper and flower shop.

—Well then, I say, let's go somewhere on Fenian Street.

So we head down Holles Street to its T-junction with Fenian Street, see the shop he mentioned standing in an open space, and turn left.

We stop at Gaffney's, Pies and Porter, *Togha Gach Bia agus Rogha Gach Dí, Fáilte Isteach*, which stands where Denzille Lane coming from Holles Street joins Fenian Street. We pass through the bar where some people are watching the UTV news and enter the lounge. There is a bar-counter and tables ranged around the wall, and joyous singing is coming from a group of girls and young men at one of the tables.

> Cross your heart, say I love you.
> Cross your heart and hope to die,
> For a very simple reason
> And here's the reason why,
> For so many hearts are broken
> By one little lie.
> Cross your heart and hope to die.

Tina's song in the Eurovision song contest back in the 70s. We sit at a table near the singers and a boy takes our orders. A couple are sitting on high stools at the counter, facing each other, holding hands, looking into each other's eyes, knees touching. She ash blonde, in blue pullover and white skirt; he balding slightly, in short-sleeved white shirt and grey trousers. Both are in their late thirties.

—We'll be off to Edinburgh in a few days, says Jim, and I tell you I'm looking forward to it.

—We have friends who have a house there, says Thérèse, and they're often away from it. It's our hideaway.

—In my business, says Jim, it's great to be able to go where no one can find you. No one ringing up to value some lost masterpiece they've found in an attic.

I say I was in Edinburgh once and that the central part is very elegant, and I thought the French influence in some of the old blocks of flats was very interesting. A reflection of the old links with France.

—I've seen it change a lot over the years, says Jim. There's a lot of lawlessness now, and the AIDS scare has made a difference. To the gays, I mean. That's a pretty big

138

scene there. You see these young fellows driving around in Mercedes.

The singers are giving us "All Kinds of Everything", Dana's song from long ago that first won the Eurovision for Ireland. How we all loved her, the little girl from Derry with the angel voice! Innocence from the North for once. The woman at the bar has her legs crossed now, and his hand is on her knee. She leans over and kisses him. He is wearing white boots, and she has blue shoes with bare legs.

—What do you think of the news from Lisburn? Jim asks me.

—Jim, I say, I no longer react to what happens in the North. I just feel quietly angry that we've had nearly twenty years of it ruining our lives, and that on present showing we're likely to have another twenty years. Now for a few days we'll have the shock/horror condemnations, and then it will be something else. And the governments will do nothing—nothing that matters or that will change anything. Conor Cruise O'Brien put it well with his "politics of the last atrocity".

—It's always an "atrocity", isn't it, says Thérèse, if it's the Provos? I hate to see words misused like that. They condemn the IRA for killing civilians, and quite rightly. They've done some terrible things. But then they hit a military target like last night, and it makes no difference. The same language is used, so that it becomes meaningless.

—I see Ray Carroll over there, I say. I wonder what he's doing in these parts. Or indeed in Dublin. You know him— the architect, sculptor, painter, poet, boat-builder, Renaissance man?

—I don't, says Jim, but I've heard of him. He lives up in the mountains somewhere?

—In Glencullen, when he's at home. But he's more at home now on Mason Island in Connemara, next to Maoinis, where I lived myself.

—How long were you there? asks Thérèse.

—Eleven years.

She asks, as so many do, whether I miss it and I say no, it was good while it lasted, but it was a period that's finished. I've moved on.

—Listen, I say, I'd better be moving on towards Westland Row.

We rise and head for the door. The woman at the bar is now caressing his left arm and putting her hand up his short shirt-sleeve. He is smiling into her eyes.

—Hello Ray, I say as I pass. Surprise, surprise! What are *we* doing here? I'm with some friends. See you on Mac Dara's Day.

—I'll be in the hotel in Cárna in the morning, he says.

Back on the street, I look around the corner of the pub up Denzille Lane to Holles Street and see back entrances of Merrion Square and Fenian Street houses, a demolished patch, a couple of mews. The street-lamps are lit and the street is empty except for a few parked cars. I have a sense that the day is ending and night beginning; a different time, another city. In the car, sitting in the front beside Jim, I can see ahead into Lincoln Place and a thin crescent moon above the Dental Hospital. We pass between the Windscreen Hospital Do Not Obstruct Day or Night and the Ginger-man pub, Ales and Porter. Donleavy must be happy to see that in his lifetime. Joyce was long dead before there was anywhere called Bloom's.

—Just turn the corner and leave me at Merrion Hall, I say to Jim. Then you're set straight for home.

Around the corner we all get out in front of the black-ened and monstrously eclectic facade of the Plymouth Brethren's meeting hall. A sign says that the sale is agreed and a poster announces, presumably for the last time, that "Salvation is of the Lord, not of works, lest any man should boast".

—Well, I say, salvation is certainly not of this work. But it

140

might look splendid with its face washed. I wonder what's going to happen it. Are you sorry you missed it, Jim? Just think what a gallery you could have in there.

—But that's funny, Thérèse says, I thought of that the other day. I was talking to Jimmy about it.

—Yes, he says, she said that's what I should buy.

—He loves it, says Thérèse.

A notice in gold lettering announces the Services: Sunday 10.30 am The Lord's Supper, 11.40 am Bible Ministry, 3.30 pm Sunday School and Bible classes, 7 pm Gospel Service, Monday 8 pm Prayer Meeting. Now no more.

—Goodbye, I say, and thanks for coming. Jim, get rid of that cold.

Jim and Thérèse go their way and I cross to the traffic island. A siren blares loudly, wildly, draws nearer, and with flashing blue lights an ambulance races towards Merrion Square. Sweny's is shuttered. I touch my pocket, feel the lemon soap, and cross Lincoln Place into Westland Row.

10.45 - 2.00 AM

NIGHT TOWN

That must be the northwest where there is still light in the sky. The dark clouds cover only part of it. In the yellow radiance of the street-lamps I walk down Westland Row. Now at last I can hear my footsteps. The sounds of a car, two cars, a bus, occur singly, and are events in the empty street. Inside the glass doors of Pearse Station Pat Sheeran is waiting for me.

—Hello Pat, you're a great man to make it. How's it going?

—Fine, he says, except in all the usual places. Nina gave me the message. What are you up to?

—Following in the steps of Leopold Bloom. This is where he'd be now. And we're heading for nighttown. By DART. We travel to Killester, the first stop beyond Amiens Street— as you'll recall, he missed his station—and then the next train back to Amiens Street, or Connolly as they call it now. Look, this is the half-cock way they do things in our great capital city. Trains still running and the ticket-office closed.

There is a man in uniform at the turnstiles selling tickets. He says the ticket-office closed at ten. He asks me and a girl beside me have we change of a pound to give change to a girl who's buying her ticket. She gives him change. I suppose this is the sort of thing that visitors to Ireland find delightfully easygoing and quaint. To Killester costs 65p each. We mount the steps to the Northbound platform.

—How long are you up for?

—Just till tomorrow, says Pat. I've an extern coming.

—Did you get that article of yours back, the one you sent me about the Cyclops? I returned it with my red-hot reactions on the back of the last page.

—No, it hadn't arrived. What did you think of it?

—Well, that's what I wrote. I said I thought it was full of wonderful "discoveries", to use your own word, but could be a bit better organised.

About fifteen people are standing on the platform or walking up and down. "Worried about your next move? Consult Lisney and Sons." At both ends the station is open to dark or darkening sky and you can feel the fresh night air moving through.

—What did you think of my delving into the Greeks and the collective unconscious, as background to an Irish topic?

—Dead on, and very illuminating. I *like* your constant probing beneath the surface of things. I know I keep to the surfaces, and you've questioned the value of that—I'll be doing it again when I write up today's odyssey. I think that does have value, both the value of tangible reality, and often the value of revelation, because people's ideas about things don't let them see or know even the surfaces. But I'm all for the other. And all the material you draw on is fine. I simply suggested a slightly tighter framework.

—Like what?

The train arrives on time, we board it and sit down. "Fare evaders will be prosecuted."

—All right, I say, I put it in three points. First, yes, Ireland, the land of Ireland, has always been depicted as a woman. Incidentally, I don't agree that there's anything reprobate in that, as you say the feminists say, and you seem to go along with. And anyhow it wasn't only men did it—look at Maud Gonne in the intro to *Servant of the Queen*—and the book's title.

143

—I don't go along with it. They're wrong. I was just taking into account what Liz Butler said at the Yeats Summer School. I must send you her paper. About its being the typical male, patriarchal thing of identifying woman with "nature".

—I suppose it's all right then for men to call their ship or car "she" because those things are man-made. Talk of nonsense eating its tail! It's the same old puritan, moralising mentality at war with art and imagination.

Below us are rows of street-lamps. Why does it remind me of coming into Belfast? Because that was my first seeing of this wondrous sight as a small child arriving there.

—OK, I say. Number two, yes again, the Irish collectively have been imaged by male figures, but not only, as you seem to suggest, negatively—as the Cyclops type, as one-eyed monsters. The Gaels were represented by two positive characters you yourself mention—Lugh *vis-à-vis* the invading Fomorians led by one-eyed Balor, and Fionn, in more popular literature. Fionn perhaps, as you say, *vis-à-vis* Goll, the one-eyed. It would be interesting by the way to find out is there any mention of Goll's being foreign.

At Tara Street station the Southbound platform is empty, but about thirty people are waiting on the Northbound one.

—Do you know, says Pat, I think I've come to understand Fionn and the Fianna. The latest Irish scholarship finds a link between them and the ancient Germanic *Männerbund*, which was a group of free-lance warriors who were always on the move. Did you see *Out of Africa*?

I nod. We have moved, and there is a glimpse of the reflecting river and the lines of lights on the quays.

—Well, do you remember that scene where this group of Masai warriors appear on a hill and walk past and disappear? That's what the Fianna were like. When I saw that, I said "That's the Fianna".

The train is trundling, almost ambling, going *ung ung ung ung-ung, ung ung ung ung-ung*, as we cross the bridges and the lines of moving traffic with headlamps lit.

—But to continue about positive male prototypes. You've got Robert Emmet and John F. Kennedy, in the sense that they were revered kitchen images of Irishness—literally displayed in kitchens.

—Right, I accept that.

—Finally, point three. The ambiguous role of the Cyclops/ Giants image in the Irish tradition. First, in the guise of Balor and the Fomorians, they are barbarous foreigners. Later they are barbarous natives—either the Irish as a whole, or a section of the Irish.

We have passed the front of the main Connolly Station building, floodlit and looking lovely, with its clock showing 11.08, crossed then over Amiens Street, and are stopping in Connolly DART station.

—If we could desist a moment, this gets good now, and I want to look out for the chain of lights around the bay. I never did this stretch before at night. I grew up in Clontarf.

About twenty people have got on, and, as we pull out of Connolly, we see an expanse of tracks, a confusion of lights from signals and other sources, and shortly we pass over a narrow line of water.

—That must have been the Royal Canal on its last lap, entering its basin, I say.

There is a track branching off to the docks, and rows of street-lamps in the East Wall area. My father had a shop there, in those mean streets, when we first came to Dublin. He told me once, if I did something again, he'd slice me up with the bacon machine. It is quite dark now. The train is picking up speed, going *ung-ung ung-ung, ung-ung ung-ung.*

—That was the Tolka river.

And now as we coast along Fairview Park we are going hell for leather. Towards the sea, pairs of red lights ascending in two parallel rows are the Poolbeg chimneys in their night dress. Towards the land, beyond the park, Fairview Road heading for the railway bridge and the coast road beyond it

145

to Clontarf and Sutton and Howth. I want to see that coastal line of lights as we cross the bridge, and I will know the bridge is coming when I see a piece of sea between the docklands and the coast road. But I am confused. A lot of sea must have been filled in because a line of lights shows a road connecting the docklands with the coast road—maybe an outlet for the East Link Bridge. And the little slice of sea I see is beyond that, and we are across the bridge with a glimpse of the road beneath, and it seems dark suddenly. No, there are scattered lights along suburban roads and we cross the bridge over Howth Road. Now it is really only blackness. We are racing along a sunken track.

—I was disappointed there. I thought we'd see more of the coastal arc from the bridge, but Clontarf Road swings out there, so we just saw a bit of it. Anyhow, this shift of the Cyclops/Giants image from barbarous foreigners to the barbarous natives, or a section of them, happened certainly under the influence of colonisation—the English view of the Irish taken over and internalised—but I have a hunch that it may have begun before that, in Gaelic Ireland.

—Oh yes, says Pat, it preceded colonisation.

—Incidentally, you mention the Citizen in *Ulysses*—the mentally one-eyed giant in the Cyclops chapter—as representing the Irish, and I'd just point out that he represents a section of the Irish, the blinkered nationalists. Stephen is also Irish, and Bloom is—and calls himself specifically—an Irishman. And by the way, Harry Blamires, in his commentary book on *Ulysses*, dwells on the one-eyed theme in Joyce and he makes an interesting remark which, in a sense, puts the Citizen in context. He reminds us that over the city of *Ulysses* towers the figure of one-eyed Nelson, embodiment of the British *imperium*. But I know, following that up would put you off your track. So we get out here. This is Killester.

On the platform we are admonished to make a sensible choice. "A colour TV licence costs £62. Fines for unlicensed TVs up to £1000." It is 11.14.

A ramp flanked on one side by bushes leads from the platform to a pedestrian bridge.

—We'll just cross over.

—Thanks, says Pat. I'll think about all that. I like the Cyclops myself, you know. I think he's a decent slob.

—Yes, I could see that. The gentle giant. And of course, leaving out the one-eyed idea, which isn't always there, you do get sympathetic treatments of the Giant or Giants. I thought of the television series, *The Incredible Hulk*, and in Doris Lessing's novel *Shikasta*, one of her science fiction books, she treats the Giants as gentle, very humane people.

—Anyway, you found it useful?

—Yes, very much so. As you can see, it set me thinking furiously. It excited me as everything you write does.

We have come down on the Southbound platform, which is as empty as the one facing us. We are in a defile between two earth banks closed at both ends by a road bridge. Small red lights mark the sides of the bridges. White lamps cast their glow on the platforms and on a line of trees above the Northbound one. A notice says: "RABHADH Ná déan foghail ar an iarnród. Don't trespass on the railway WARNING." We start walking up and down.

—It's supposed to come at 11.24. So apart from all that, what have you been up to?

—Well, I've been doing some very interesting research today into the apparitions at Knock and I think that maybe I've got confirmation for a hypothesis about them. But first I'll tell you about this conference I was at in the States recently. I went over to a literary conference, and left it and went to this gathering of technoshamans in Kentucky. It disguised itself as a metaphysical conference. It was run by a Dublin Jew whose father was Russian and mother Irish. His name is Peter Moscow. He identifies very strongly with Bloom, and looks like I imagine Bloom to have been. He's a large fat man with a waddle, in exile in this pretty desperate place, Louisville, Kentucky. So he developed these powers of clairvoyance and so on, and set up this company, Holistic Philosophy Consultants Inc. He invites all the crazies of America to come to Kentucky once a year and do their stuff. The highlight of this year was bringing over from West Germany, from Aachen, a group of scientists or pseudo-scientists—I couldn't quite figure out which—who were in touch with the dead. They had done it by means of television, which was switched on to no particular channel—a vacant channel—with a video camera placed in front of it and the whole thing wired up into a video-recorder—I don't understand the technology of it, but it seemed to have to do with getting instant images. They had videos of their experiments, and among other things they showed Romy Schneider, and Albert Einstein in a cloth cap.

—Is Romy Schneider dead?

—She's dead for a long time. They had images of these people moving, and even speaking, though the words were not intelligible. There was also somebody from Luxembourg there, a member of the Department of Justice with his wife. One day he had lifted up the phone and had been spoken to a dead friend, and then messages from this friend were left on their answering machine.

—How did you find out about this? How were you clued into the network?

We hear a train approaching from the northern direction, and turning, see its red lights. Can it be our train, early? A freight train passes, waggons of metal drums. In the sky to the northwest there is still a red glow from the departed sun, and in the southern sky the red glow of Dublin by night.

—When I was teaching in Austin in Texas a few years ago, I had seen advertisements for it. One of the things I had determined to do when I got to America was to get to some kind of new frontier. I'm not interested in, say, the guerilla war frontier, or the military frontier, or a civil rights frontier, because they seem to me to have been covered. So what I discovered in America was a sort of psychic frontier where all sorts of crazy things were happening. And this I wanted to explore—sceptically, of course. I went to the Kentucky conference when I was in Texas, and then again this year, to get the whole picture.

—Excuse me a moment, but do you get why they put that shaggy dog in the advertisement for de luxe emulsion paint?

—Shaggy dog means cosy home.

—OK. Now what was this conference actually called?

—The Seth and Metaphysical Conference. Seth is an otherworld being who up until recently was dictating all sorts of messages to people. They think of him as a psyche, or what they now call a "channel"—a channel for these messages.

A girl with long, blonde hair in a leather jacket and white trousers has walked onto the platform opposite. It is 11.24 and all is silence. It strikes me that I have misread the time-table and that we are to be stranded here all night. New twist to Bloomsday.

—Just a minute, Pat, while I check.

I extract the time-table from my plastic bag and embark on a laborious search through the lines of small figures. 11.24, yes, Killester for Connolly. Then we hear it coming, see it, and in a few seconds it is stopped in front of us. It is almost empty. I press a button to open the doors and, as we sit down, it moves again. A magnified man's voice says, "Ladies and gentlemen, this train terminates at Connolly Station."

—A while ago you called these people technoshamans, if I heard you right.

—Yes, that's my own word, and I use it because it seems to me that the worldview of these people, the world model in which they situate themselves, is actually a pre-modern one. But this is coupled with the use of the most sophisticated modern technology—computers, television and so on. To give you another example of it, Pat Robertson, the erstwhile candidate for the presidency of the USA—before Dukakis emerged, in the early stages. One of his claims to fame was that he had stopped a hurricane that was heading for New York. He was a fundamentalist preacher and a serious contender for the presidency, down South. He was also the founder of a sixty million dollar a year communications industry. He was no fool, he wasn't some sort of hick.

— So this for you is shaman technology.

I check the view of the coast road as we pass over it again, but it is no better. Dog roses, I've got the term. I am thinking of the red and white wild roses that I saw on the embankment next us as we walked along the platform.

—Yes, it is the combination of two totally different worlds, which seem actually to function pretty well together, but which in theory ought not to.

—You could imagine, following this out logically, our modern scientific age differently organised.

— Absolutely.

— Not according to rationalism or, as it's put, the Enlightenment heritage.

— Not according to the Enlightenment heritage, in fact the Enlightenment heritage isn't necessary for this. I've seen this before in Findhorn in Scotland, in the New Age commune there, where for example they invite the nature spirits in to help them in their garden, while at the same time they use very sophisticated computer networking to distribute their publications. So it seems to me that the Enlightenment rationality and empiricism are not actually necessary in order to use our technology and to profit by it.

—That's fascinating. It's the kind of thing that struck me in another sense when I was in Jamshedpur in India, and I went one day to the steel works there, which is the biggest in India, if not in Asia. It was on a Hindu religious festival. And what I saw was lines of people with holy paint on their faces, and wearing wreaths of flowers, snaking among the machinery. And there was a platform set up in an open space with a ritual and dance taking place on it. In other words, the industrial work-place combined with religion. You know in Europe how, during the industrial revolution, work and religion went different—

Pat, who has been shaking his head up and down vigorously, says:

—Yeah, yeah, but—

But we have arrived in Connolly and have got up to leave with the six other passengers. One young man is carrying a viola-sized musical instrument case. Was he playing in a hotel in Howth? "Carpet City 42 Talbot Street, Discount for Dart Users". We set off along a white-tiled echoing passage.

—Yes, but there is a problem about that, he says, and I think there's a very important distinction to be made. There is a similar situation, for instance, in the Iran-Iraqi war where you have men with medieval minds flying supersonic jets. The problem about this kind of application of it is that it's totally uncreative. Your Hindu using the technology, your Islamic fundamentalist using the technology, is unable to develop it. He's simply exploiting it, he's parasitical on it. Whereas in the American scene they are both creatively developing the technology, and at the same time have this other mindset. There's a very important difference. And in fact the whole of the Islamic world is at this stage parasitical on Western technology. They even decry Western technology, while using it. They never creatively develop it. I think V.S. Naipaul's book *Among the Believers* is a fundamental text as regards this. He travels the Islamic countries and he constantly remarks on their parasitical use of the technology—which they're not even able to repair.

—Yes.

We are on Amiens Street opposite Lloyd's shuttered pub, a couple of hundred yards away from the main station exit opposite Talbot Street. A poster in the DART station doorway says "Exhibition in the Dublin Camera Club, Lr Baggot St, Millennium My City, Pat Casey". And in Connolly's shoe-shop I can have my children's shoes correctly fitted on an electronic foot guage.

—Now this, Pat continues, is not the situation in the States, or it's not the situation let's say in England, where you have people of immense mathematical and technological sophistication at the same time fitting this into a totally other worldview.

—Yeah.

—So it does seem that it's necessary to have passed through the Enlightenment heritage to make a creative transformation of it.

—Yes, I get you. To be practical a moment, Lloyd's pub there is on the corner of Foley Street, which used to be called Montgomery Street. It gave its nick-name, the Monto, to the entire brothel area. And Beaver Street joins Foley Street just behind Lloyd's. So we'll be doing a circle, so to speak, and coming back there.

—We head up Talbot Street now then?

—Right.

I need tobacco. Lloyd's is shuttered. The Mascot, Tobacconist, Newsagent, is closed. Mullett's pub next door to Lloyd's has its door closed, but the lights are on.

—I need tobacco. Let's see can I get it in Mullett's.

Half-way across the street we pause as three last buses, 28, 30, and 42, pass in succession in the direction of Clontarf. I knock twice on Mullett's door and a man puts his head out. No, they have no pipe tobacco. There seems to be an unwritten rule forbidding pubs to stock pipe tobacco, but since I can think of no basis for it, I keep hoping for an exception. In vain so far, but it helps me work off my frustration. At the railway bridge, just after Terry Rogers Bookmaker, Cleary's pub, which was once the Signal House, still has its neon sign lit in the window. But the gate on the porch is closed. We continue towards the North Star Hotel—Vacancies. Its Bianconi restaurant, adjacent, is open until 3 am. To enter you ring a bell. It's the only late-night place in these parts. Across the street a guard has stopped two bright-faced boys of about 12 and 15 who have come out of Sheriff Street. He is questioning them, tapping their clothes, evidently searching them.

—They've come out of Sheriff Street, I say. You've heard of Sheriff Street. You've heard how they're wondering what to do about its being a stone's throw from the swish Custom House Quay development, with its international men of finance and posh apartments. I suppose the guard's after drugs or something. It saddens me that. Maybe they're up to something, but maybe they're not. One way or another they're suspect because of where they live. Not much chance there for youthful innocence.

Released, the boys cross the street, start running as fast they can, and disappear around the corner into Talbot Street. There are few pedestrians around, but cars, homeward bound after pub, cinema or theatre, pour from the direction of Butt Bridge and Abbey Street or head left towards Matt Talbot Bridge. Let's see has the North Star tobacco. A man bars my way into the bar. No, I'm not looking for drink.

—Have you pipe tobacco?

—Don't stock it, he says, wagging his head sideways.

—By the way, I say to Pat, about your Cyclops piece, I forgot to mention Daniel O'Connell. He was a Cyclops—big-bodied, Gaelic, Catholic, rural—who bestrode both worlds. A brilliant lawyer, European liberal, freemason, Benthamite, all the metropolitan things, while remaining rooted in his cyclopean soil. That's why he towers, literally, in Irish history.

—I get it, says Pat. I'll think about that. Another thing I wanted to say to you about the States was that it seemed to me that the so-called "romantic Ireland" is actually there. That it may well be—it was a Pole who pointed this out to me—that the great current American interest in an alternative world, in otherworldly beings, for example, the very widespread interest in extra-terrestrials—extra-terrestrials are a given fact, eighty per cent of the population believes in them, and it's not a problem for them—that all this is actually the influence of the Irish emigration. It is simply a different language. Fairies are now extra-terrestrials. In other words, the impact of Irish emigration may not in the end have been just political. It may have been the *pisreogs* as well.

We have come to the corner of Talbot Street, opposite the main station, and stand looking across at Grainger's pub and another Terry Rogers betting shop.

—Not quite the same point, I say, but earlier in the day I met Bruce Arnold in his office, being interviewed by this Canadian radio man about Yeats. And the Canadian asked him and me about the situation of the Celtic thing in Ireland today. And I said it is there in a residual way from the Gaelic League and Kuno Meyer epoch. But it's also there in a new way, slotted into the Alternative Life thing by English, French, Germans, Americans.

—Absolutely, it's got a whole cosmopolitan dimension, like Irish music. And there are clairvoyants in the States who see a connection between the Red Indians and the Celts. But that's another day's work.

—We'll cross over here.

On the other side we turn right into a street of silence. Right up to O'Connell Street it is empty of traffic, though some is crossing it at Gardiner Street. Two or three cars are parked, and I think they will not be there for long. The shops have put on their night dress of metal roller shutters, some opaque, some of the punched-lath kind that you can see through. Security firms, armoured vans, burglar alarms, guard dogs, metal shutters, more policemen with more gadgetry—it has become that sort of city. Virtuous self-restraint, mocked and waning since the 60s, has cost a great deal of money to replace. Carpet City Carpet and Furniture Superstore. So there it is.

—Look at that, says Pat. FURNITURAMA.

The letters, two feet high, extend for nearly twenty yards.

—That's where the New Electric Cinerama used to be, I say. *The Sound of Music* ran for months there.

A train rumbles across the bridge above us. A blowzy woman with blonde hair and bloated body, wild eyes staring, waddles past. Connolly's shoe-shop with its electronic foot guage, specialists in Irish Dancing Shoes. A lone taxi passes. Cries of girls come from Spencer Row. Furniture this, and wallpapers that, and carpets.

—It seems to be the place to come when you've bought a new house, says Pat.

We are at Olhausen's, Pork Butcher's, which has a see-through shutter.

—Do you notice anything odd? I ask.

—No, says Pat. What?

—"Established 1935"—that's odd, isn't it?

—Very odd when you come to think of it.

—At Lowry's pub there, that's where he crossed.

At Lowry's we cross into totally empty Corporation Street. After a couple of derelict houses, a high grey wall runs along the left side. Tall lamp-posts with extended arms drop circles of light. What we used to call 1984 country. Instinctively we walk in the centre of the street. A young man comes running from behind us and turns the corner into Foley Street. Another urgent errand of the night. A sudden group of trees. What are they doing here? Small trees behind a railing extend down the left side of empty, cobble-stoned Foley Street. Backs and a few warehouse signs on the other side.

—My goodness, this is grim, says Pat.

The high grey wall is Eason's Cash and Carry. "Up the Provos", and beneath it, urine trailing away. More trees on the other side of Walsh's shuttered shop. Our footsteps are echoing, plip, plop. A block of Corporation flats behind a railing. Balconies on the corner flats. The pebble-dash plaster has peeled in patches. There are flowers in some windows. "For under socialism the workers won't only have bread in their bellies. They will have flowers in the windows of their houses." Thus Tony Cronin, a star of the Literary and Historical Debating Society when I was in my first year in college, finished a ringing speech and left me spellbound. On the left-hand corner with Railway Street, a bleak closed pub with narrow windows. Hubbub inside, two cars outside. A dog barks from the balcony of a first-floor flat.

We turn right into empty Railway Street between blocks of flats.

—Hey mister! Who are you looking for?

It is a woman's voice from above on the right, and looking up we see two women on a third-floor balcony.

—Bella Cohen's, I say.

Her house was over to the left there, where the flats have continuous balconies running around an enclosed square.

—Never heard of her. Are ye sure she lives round here?

Lights in the flats, rows and rows of curtained windows, secret homes up there. A baby crying. Now there is the high, black wall of a convent on the left and a furnace chimney rising behind it.

—These flats could be in Warsaw or somewhere like that, says Pat.

—Just imagine in the old days, the crowd of men along here, women in the windows and at doors, calling like that one now. Drunks being ejected at doorways.

There is a cross of white bricks embedded in the convent wall, and another some distance beyond it. "Stop Extradition". "Brits Out". "Bobby Sands RIP".

—No wonder, says Pat, the bourgeoisie fear the Provos. It's a class thing, isn't it, dressed up in moral rhetoric.

The flats end and there is an open railinged space transected by a dirty grey wall with peeling plaster. Inside the wall, next the flats, three cars are parked. Two women are chatting on a balcony. A lane opens on the right.

—This, I say, is Beaver Street where he helped Stephen to his feet.

We turn into it between the railinged space and a corrugated iron fence, enclosing emptiness, which runs for more than half its length. "Cops are liers" on the grey wall with peeling plaster. Over the warehouse roofs at the end of the lane, a floodlit Florentine tower of Connolly Station shows. Not only around it but all over, the sky is starless. Towards the city-centre it glows red. On an old two-storey house the words "James J. Daly Brush Manufacturer" read consolingly. Like discovering the imprint of a human hand in a cave not

157

opened since Palaeolithic times. It is dark here beside this high, white wall because the lamp is out of action, but we are at the end of the lane, at cobbled Foley Street. Two guards are approaching along it, one of them talking into his radio. On the corner, in the recessed gateway of Ferrum Trading Company Steel Stockholders, a boy is kissing a girl tenderly.

Back on Amiens Street, we turn right at Lloyd's along the footpath which we walked half an hour ago. A woman passes in multicoloured shawl, grasping a half-empty bottle of a colourless liquid.

—I'm glad I saw that, says Pat. What a transformation!

—Yes, the new state made a clean sweep. I don't know if you've noticed that all revolutionaries are puritans. They must prove their moral superiority to the regime they have overthrown. And they always begin by getting rid of the prostitutes, turning them into decent girls plying useful trades.

Mullet's still has its lights on. Cleary's porch gate has been opened to let the last drinkers out.

—I was thinking, I say, since there's nothing open late around here, that we'd go to Joys night-club on Baggot Street.

—Fine by me, says Pat. Do you know it?

—I go there now and again. We'll look for a taxi around Store Street.

Connolly Station is very beautiful with its pillars and loggia and towers and lamps. The buses have stopped, and there are only cars now after the pubs. We cross Talbot Street. The long high wall flanking the ramp to the station runs along the other side of Amiens Street. We pass an office-block and read on a black iron gate "City Morgue No Parking Day or Night".

—Says something about death, doesn't it, says Pat. You know not the day nor the hour.

—I'd love to see inside a morgue. I've seen them in films. I'd like to see the dead lying on those trays or slabs.

The Master Mariner, Pub Food, Lounge is on the corner where we turn into Store Street. The bus station, six storeys of glass, across from us. Another heavy iron door leads to the Coroner's Court No Parking Day or Night, and here is the famous or notorious Store Street Garda Station where all human life comes all through the night. Two plain-clothes men emerge and go to one of the parked cars. A helmeted guard on a motorbike comes to a stop between two police vans. The Kylemore Bakery on night shift. There's a taxi standing outside Busáras, but it seems abandoned.

—I forgot of course, I say. There are always taxis here when the bus station's open, but there's no reason for them to be here when it's closed. We'll walk on. We're sure to catch a roving one. What you were telling me about that conference and that American scene was very interesting.

Through the closed doors of the bus station I see empty benches and the Information Desk. Ahead of us the white, floodlit back of the Custom House through trees.

—There's an apocalyptic aspect of it which I think is dangerous, says Pat. As well as the acceptance of the existence of extra-terrestrials and what they call implantations—the extra-terrestrials are trying to breed a new race, women all over the States are waking up with pregnancies, they go into regression hypnosis and describe the experience of technological rape by these otherworld beings, then the foetus goes away and they tell under hypnosis how it was removed by the aliens—just as all this is accepted, so is the notion of a great cleansing that is about to occur, and can be made to occur. The assumption is that consciousness is primary, creative, creates reality, so that belief creates reality, and if everyone believes that Apocalypse Now is on the way, then it will happen.

We are on a traffic island in Beresford Place watching the headlights move towards us from Butt Bridge. The white night-ghost of Liberty Hall looms high. All the taxis we see are occupied. From Abbey Street the blaring horn of an ambulance sounds, and the stopped cars shift to make way for it as it approaches and passes, all blue lights and searing noise.

—The apocalypse was imagined for a while to be an atomic one, I say.

—It's no longer imagined as atomic, that's gone. The Cold War thing is gone.

—Is it now the sun dancing, the third secret of Fatima to be revealed?

—No. I heard the third secret of Fatima at the conference, it was revealed at the conference. I'll get onto that. No, the apocalypse they expect takes the shape of the California earthquake scenario, climatic changes, earth changes.

Skirting the Custom House railings, we are approaching Butt Bridge.

—A freezing over, the greenhouse effect? Let's cross to the other corner of the bridge, and we'll have a chance of a taxi from two directions.

—It's more the earth sort of shrugging off all the pollutants, man's impositions on it. There's a popular acceptance of the to-some-degree scientific hypothesis that the earth is a living being, the Gaia hypothesis. I don't know if you're familiar with this. James Lovelock, a major scientist at the moment, has put it forward. The earth is best understood as a living being, Gaia, that does everything except reproduce itself. It breathes, defecates and so on. And the popular version is that this Gaia will simply unload itself and renew itself through devastating earthquakes, earth changes, mountains falling and the like. Another widespread idea that goes with this is that the people on the other side, as they call them, are ready for a massive irruption into this world.

—The undead?

It is a quarter past twelve on the Custom House clock. A freight train trundles across the Loop Line bridge probably heading for Rosslare.

—The undead. They are working on their technology to communicate with us and will break into one of the national networks and announce their presence.

An empty taxi comes along Eden Quay and stops when I signal it. We get into the back seat. I say Joys, and he heads off along Custom House Quay for the Matt Talbot Bridge.

—These are not beliefs, says Pat, that are confined to the crazy. They are very widespread beliefs.

—And how did the third secret of Fatima arise? The reason I'm interested is that I saw on television, the Late Late or something, the Portuguese woman married in New York who is the bearer of the third secret. She was one of the children who saw the apparitions.

—That's a Garabandal secret you're talking about. She was Spanish.

—No, she was talking about Fatima. She said she would reveal the secret on a certain date, which she must keep to herself, and it will be followed by such a manifest showing of God's power in the world that nobody can but accept His existence. She said this as a very sober woman, who has children and goes about her housework.

We have passed the *Lady Patricia* at her moorings, turned into the City Quay housing estate, and are heading for Westland Row.

—I think you're confused, says Pat. But perhaps it will all fall into place. Anyhow there's this guy, Gerry Bowman, who has got a show on West Coast television. He's a channeller, that is, he goes into this trance-like state and John the Apostle speaks to him. He talks about the "man Jesu". He is a very unprepossessing poor white, and if he has any marks of spirituality I could not discover them. The whole channelling scene is extremely murky, and very questionable, and I would think a very dangerous scene.

—A channeller is someone who transmits for some otherworld being, is that right?

—Right. When Bowman is performing, his face changes, his voice changes, and he strides up and down, and speaks with great authority. Now all this is being recorded on video camera. So suddenly he says, "Turn off the cameras. I'm going to reveal the third secret of Fatima". And all the cameras, recording equipment and so on are switched off. Then he says, "The third secret of Fatima was very simple". You know of course that when the Pope heard it he fell into a faint, and you know all the mythology, and you can imagine me, with an Irish Catholic background, my ears out like this—at last! I had been terrified in my youth by the rumours about it, by my mother and parents and all the rest of it. So he says the third secret of Fatima is as follows. A major pope—Bowman himself would be from a Protestant fundamentalist background—would be assassinated in St Peter's and this would precipitate the Third World War, just as the First World War had been precipitated by this guy being shot in some remote Serbian province. Now the fact is, he says, this has already happened. The Pope, the present one, has already being shot in St Peter's Square. But due to the rising spirituality in the world, the change going on in people's consciousness, he survived, and the Third World War did not happen, and is not going to happen. The world has turned a corner and we are entering an age of peace. And by the way, and quite apart from that, we do live in very remarkable days. Maybe never before in history has peace been so widespread.

There were three whores on the side of Merrion Square we passed along, and one car was stopped, negotiating. We have reached the traffic light at the Baggot Street corner.

—All of this, I say to Pat, has been rising in America probably antecedent to, or at least coincident with, the Gorbachov period in Russia. Isn't that right? I mean there was a *Weltgeist* at work there.

—Yes, that's right, with the emphasis on *geist*.

Incredibly, people are still standing with drinks outside Doheny and Nesbitt's. A short distance beyond it the taxi stops and we get out. It is twenty-five past twelve.

—Just across here, I say.

We descend the iron stairs to the heavy iron door with the spy-hole in the basement. I ring, it opens and Des Fox smiles a greeting.

—Welcome, Desmond, good to see you.

—How are you, Des. This is Pat Sheeran from Galway.

—Welcome, says Des Fox. It's fairly quiet so far, but it should liven up.

A song, "It doesn't matter any more", is coming from beyond the inner door. I hand my coat and bag to Des and we pass through the door into a room dimly lit with ochre light, where a long bar, shiny black, curves to meet us. Two men and two women are sitting at it a few stools apart, and the bar-girl is chatting with the men. The light is coming from shaded wall-lamps and from the tops of square, reflecting pillars on the edge of the dance-floor. Multicoloured ceiling lights are flashing, lazily, on the polished surface. We cross it and mount three steps to the raised area where there are tables, each with a lit candle shaded by red glass. At one of these, in the centre of the floor, is a mixed party of five, and near them, at a small table on the side next the bar, two men, with champagne between them, are talking Spanish. We sit at a table for two just behind them, the only table with a naked candle. A pretty girl in a bronze-coloured blouse and short black skirt comes to us with the wine-list, which Pat takes. Her hair is piled high, and her eyes under their mascara'd lashes are attentive.

—Is white OK? I ask Pat. I know an agreeable one.

Pat says fine, so I say to the girl:

—We'll have the Piesporter. Oh, and bring me a cigar, a Corona.

When she is gone, Pat says:

—Are you getting a bottle? They're very dear.

—You have to get a bottle. Their only other drink is port at £4 a glass. I've heard it debated which is better—a cover charge of, say, £7, like they have in some places outside the city, and the wine at seven or eight pounds, or no cover charge and the wine £16. But this is the only place I come occasionally. I like it. Especially on a quiet night like tonight. On Friday and Saturday it's crowded, especially Friday.

Now there is disco music and one must raise one's voice a bit to be heard, but it is not aggressively loud, not blaring. I notice that in the back part beyond the gapped partition wall, where you can get away from the music, a lone couple are sitting talking quietly. The party of five near us, two women and three men, are speaking a mixture of French and of foreign-accented English. More people are arriving at the bar, and Frank Conway, the owner, is ushering some people to his table at the wall. The girl returns, hands me a cigar, and pours the wine. I light the cigar from the candle.

—Before we leave those things you've been telling me about, I say, I'd like to hear what you yourself think of it all. Where's the line? Is it simply a great wave of superstition? I think it's fascinating that a Dublin Jew should be its impresario, so to speak.

—Well, in Louisville, he was, says Pat. Oh there were other incredibly crazy things I haven't told you about. But it's all perfectly intelligible within the terms of traditional metaphhysics. They are tapping into what has always been dismissed by all the great traditions, and rightly dismissed, as the intermediary level. If you take the world as being constituted by *spiritus*, *animus* and *anima*, the *animus* being the ordinary physical and psychological world, then it's *anima* we're talking about, the intermediary realm of soul to which ghosts, tupas and clairvoyants belong.

—Ghosts and what?

—Tupas. One of the great feats of the Tibetan lama is to create a human being imaginatively, a human being who can actually speak to you.

164

—I didn't know that. I see.

—And the next part of the exercise is for him to reabsorb this projection. One of the readings that these people would have of, say, Communism, is that it is a collective, monstrous creation, as it were, in the psychic realm. When Marx says in the *Communist Manifesto*, "A spectre is haunting Europe", these people would say, yes, you're fucking right, and you created it.

—So they're able to translate their American anti-Communism onto this level?

—Well, actually it wasn't an American who said that, it was a Lithuanian I read.

—Oh, that makes a difference.

We both laugh. Pat says he likes the wine. There are about ten people at the bar now, and two couples are dancing to big-band music. Occasional shouts and loud laughs break through the music.

—But anyhow, says Pat, in terms of Christian metaphysics, they are simply into this intermediate realm which is always deceitful and lying, a place where the souls after death are confused.

—The place of gibbering shades?

—Yes, precisely. This is my reading of it.

—You know, I've long thought that *Ulysses* is a portrait of that place, just as our other Great Novel, *Cré na Cille*, by Máirtín Ó Cadhain, is the meandering talk of the dead in a village graveyard.

—But however awful and gauche and all the rest of it this is, I see it as a first step. I think there are historical precedents for people experimenting with this sort of thing, finding its futility, and then going on to the real thing.

At Frank Conway's table, a squat, authoritative man is eating a meal and holding forth to Frank and another man about house prices in the south of Spain. The other, younger man has the tough face and unblinking eyes of a mercenary.

A dreamy girl is leaning on his shoulder dozing. Occasionally, she wakes, sips from her glass, listens briefly to the talk, replaces her head, and dozes off again.

—You're reminding me of something, I say. I always touch base with the Roman world. I have great empathy with it. They had their modern age long before us and we can inform ourselves very well about it. Around the time of the transition from Republic to Empire and for a century after that, it was all the thing, in fashionable circles, to dismiss the supernatural. One was modern and enlightened and all that, and the gods were for the peasants. But then in the course of the second century, an enormous wave of religiosity and superstition swept the world again. And it was in this context, ultimately, that Constantine established Christianity. There was a re-religising of an atheised society.

—Yes. This is what's happening in the States. It's a re-sacralisation. The transcendental is very much in again, even if, for the present, in a debased form. What I would think of as the paradigm for it is the Celtic Renaissance here, with Yeats and George Russell. I mean, they began by dabbling in the stupidly occult, in the fairies, in superstition, and going to Soho to mediums, but they ended up reading the Hindu classics, going to Sri Purohitswami and so on. Of course, there is a whole other America which is kind of liberal and so on, which detests all this and sees it as aberrant. Most American intellectuals are mad fucking socialists and feminists, extremely uninteresting people, mouthing the gibberish ten or twenty years later of European intellectuals. But in this area of exploration I've been talking about, America is ahead. Listen, is there a phone here? I'd like to call Nina.

I tell him where the phone is, and he goes off. Frank Conway, who has already greeted me with a smile and a hand-wave, comes over, asks how I'm keeping and says they haven't seen me for some time.

166

—I'm keeping well, I say, because I've been going to bed early. You yourself seem none the worse for the night-time wear and tear. Tell me who's the man holding forth at you table?

—Terry Rogers. You don't know him?

—No, I say. So that's the fabled Terry Rogers, gambler *extraordinaire*. We passed two of his shops earlier tonight.

—Are they looking after you? asks Frank.

But before I have time to answer, there is a flickering of light from the back area, and Frank, noticing it, looks towards the door, excuses himself, and goes off in that direction. The girl in the bronze blouse picks up our two glasses and the bottle, places them on a tray, moves quickly to the Spanish-speakers and does likewise, and I see another girl gathering the glasses and bottles from the two tables near us. At the party of five's table, eyes follow her in amazement.

—*Mais qu'est-ce que c'est que ça?* exclaims one of the women, the one wearing glasses.

And she looks towards me questioningly because I look native.

—*C'est la police*, I say.

Now all ten eyes are turned towards me, and I realise that my bald statement must sound alarming. But how to explain that all of Dublin's night-clubs are strictly illegal, as Dublin's and the Republic's local radio stations are blatantly illegal, but that nevertheless they exist in large numbers and openly, and are flourishing businesses in whose premises one is safe? It is also running through my head that it is very unusual, not to say unmannerly, that the guards should put in an appearance so early in the night. So I say, speaking very clearly:

—The police do not like people drinking after midnight without eating.

But as I say it, the waitress returns to their table and deftly replaces the glasses in order. Our girl returns and does the same for Pat and me.

167

—False alarm, she says.

—False alarm, I say to our bewildered visitors, smiling all over my face. Are you on holidays in Ireland?

They reply—and they point to the two Spanish-speakers, including them—that they are stamp-dealers who have been attending a stamp fair in Dublin. They introduce themselves as Francine (she of the spectacles) and Jacques, Eva and Helmut who are Germans, and Sven from Sweden. For good measure, Miguel and Raimundo, from Madrid and Valencia, introduce themselves too. I rise to shake each hand in turn, mentioning my own first name, which they find odd—the name, I mean.

—Welcome all, I say. *Fáilte, Willkommen, soyez les bienvenus, bienvenidos.*

When I sit down again, Pat has already resumed his seat.

—Showing off your languages? he says. How'd you get talking to them?

—An incident occurred while you were away, I say. An imagined garda raid, which turned out to be a false alarm. We were thrown together in the commotion. I'm sorry there's no Albanian there, they've a wonderful word for *welcome*. Did you get Nina?

—Yes, he says. She's fine. I was filling her in on my research today, this geological theory I'm exploring about the apparitions at Knock.

—I won't ask you about that, I say, not this time. I'll be taking you home by taxi. You're at your sister's I suppose? But first we will pay a visit to Leopold and Molly and wish them good-night.

Fat Helmut catches my eyes, raises his hand, rises from his chair with some difficulty, and takes a couple of steps towards me.

—We have a question, he says.

I go over to their table.

—We were wondering, he says, what this word means, Bloomsday. We see it in many places. Blooms are flowers, yes?

The faces regard me expectantly. I pause and recollect myself. This requires succinctness and a certain solemnity.

—Just a moment, I say.

I return to my seat and say to Pat:

—I've been called on to preach the gospel of Bloom and I intend to do it like Peter on the first Pentecost, so that each will hear it in his own tongue, Parthians, Medes and Elamites, and visitors from Stockholm. Infuse me with the Holy Ghost.

Pat smiles and says:

—Fo fa fum.

I take a sip of wine and return to the stamp-dealers.

—*Es war an diesem Tag, dem 16. juni, im Roman* Ulysses *von James Joyce, dass der Dubliner Jude, Leopold Bloom, seine Odyssee durch Dublin machte.*

—*C'était ce jour-ci, le 16 juin, dans le roman* Ulysse *de James Joyce, que le juif dublinois, Léopold Bloom, a fait son odyssée à travers Dublin.*

—*Det var dag, den 16 juni, i romanen* Ulysses *av James Joyce, denna som Dublinjuden, Leopold Bloom, gjorde sin odyssé genom Dublin.*

The faces smile and Sven reminds me of the actor, Max von Sydow. Helmut exclaims:

—*Wie sprachbegabt!*

But he has heard nothing yet. Bald Miguel, in open-necked, polka-dot shirt, and dark, slim Raimundo in blue business suit, have been absorbed in their own conversation, unaware of these developments. So they are surprised when I turn to them and say:

—*Fué en este día, el 16 de junio, en la novela* Uliseo *de James Joyce, que el judío dublinés, Leopold Bloom, ha hecho su odiseo a través de Dublín.*

Feeling like a tight-rope walker out of practice and breath who has just reached the other side, I make for the wings.

—Francine, I say, would you like to dance?

She glances at Jacques and says *oui*. It is a slow dance, which suits me. A rhythmic shuffle gets me by. She is wearing a red trouser-suit and her eyes have a piercing look, presumably from peering at stamps. She dances well. There are only three other couples on the floor, so we have space to move around.

—Francine, I say, my friend and I go soon to Mr Bloom's house. He and his wife, Molly are sleeping after his long day. I want an international delegation to wish them good-night. When you are ready to go, I can take four people in the taxi. One French, I hope you. One German, one Spanish, one Swede.

—I will tell them, she says.

Shortly after, they say yes, they want to come and they are ready; so we leave. Several taxis are waiting outside. All of the stamp-dealers want to come, and they will take a second taxi, but I get my prescribed delegation to come with Pat and myself. Raimundo, Sven, and Helmut go in the back with Pat, Francine in the front between the driver and me.

—Eccles Street, I say to the taximan, but we want to go by Butt Bridge and Gardiner Street.

That sends us on a detour by way of Fitzwilliam Square. The empty streets are lit by yellow globes suspended from tall silver posts. The parking meters standing in line, without cars to hide them, seem bereft and absurd, like prehistoric animals. The clock at Louis Copeland Tailor said five to two. A man pushing a bike, a luminous strap around his waist and bandolier-like up his back, stops, takes a cigarette from his mouth, and looks up at the sky. We are properly on the route only when we have crossed Baggot Street further up and are heading down the east side of Merrion Street towards the facade of Holles Street Hospital. A young woman in white raincoat walks quickly, her head down. Lights from basement areas illuminate the ground floors of the Georgian houses. Dark shrubbery and trees hide the park where the flowers sleep, waiting for the sun's return to blow their trumpets. I realise I have forgotten to pay for the wine in Joys, but I can settle that another time. We get a green light into Holles Street and it is green again at Fenian Street as we turn left. Right then through Upper Sandwith Street, and under the railway bridge, and we are stopped by a red at Pearse Street. On the hoarding opposite, a child's pensive face, chin on hand. "May all your troubles be little ones. Insurance Corporation of Ireland". The others are stopped behind us, and there is another taxi to our right.

—Is it far? asks Francine.

—No, I say, and especially at this time of night. We just cross the river, go up a long street, and we're there.

It is all green traffic-arrows along Pearse Street, and as we drive through Tara Street to Butt Bridge.

—What is its name? asks Francine, pointing to the river.

I tell her. The water is dead calm, the tide high, and O'Connell Bridge, with its reflection, forms three slender white ellipses. Where we turn into Lower Gardiner Street, three green signposts, "Belfast, Derry, Cavan", evoke the distant North. The Bed and Breakfast neons make the street bright. Turning towards the back seat, but so that Francine can hear, I say:

—Perhaps you know, but anyhow at the end of *Ulysses* Leopold Bloom walks up this street from the river to his house with his friend, Stephen. His wife, Molly is waiting for him in bed.

—What is the Corporation in Spanish? asks Pat, who has been explaining things.

—The *Municipio* should do, I say.

After Talbot Street the broad empty expanse of Middle Gardiner Street rises up before us under yellow globes on silver posts and with all the traffic lights showing green. Mountjoy Square, and a young man in black leather jacket and blue jeans is walking with a girl in denim by the park railing.

—Did you do good business at the stamp fair? I ask Francine.

—A little, she says, but it was good fun.

Left now into Gardiner Place as a man in dark glasses comes down the steps of the Dergvale Hotel. At the turn for Temple Street the lights stop us. A Garda car is facing us, and behind it the big perpendicular sign of Barry's Hotel spells the words in red letters on gleaming white.

Belvedere College in darkness. I think of the Latin class and Father Byrne. Two women standing talking outside the Corporation flats. The big furniture lorry is still there, just before St George's Church. And here is the James Joyce Lounge at the bottom of Eccles Street. All in order. I intend no complications. Bloom lives for tonight in No. 75, which looks domestic with its lace curtains. The Mater Private Hospital is gently illuminated by hidden lamps along its base. I cannot see the silver traceries of the street-lamps that I admired this morning, only their yellow globes suspended and their silver posts.

—If you'd just stop on the left here for a moment, I say to the driver, outside No. 75.

He does so, and glancing back, I see the other taxi stopping behind us. I open my window.

—Good night, Leopold. Remember me wherever you are. Good night, Molly. *Codhladh sámh*!

—*Bonne nuit et de bons rêves*, says Francine, leaning across me to look out. Raimundo has opened the back window.

—*Buenas noches, Leopold y Molly. Con mucho amor.*

—*God natt, sov gott*, says Sven.

Helmut and Pat have got out and are standing looking at the houses over the roof of the taxi.

—*Herr Bloom und Frau Molly*, Helmut says, *schlafen Sie gut!*

—Poldy, y'ould bollocks, cries Pat, don't you know how to lie in a bed?

—Look, I see him, says Raimundo. His face is at the window, at the top.

Francine leans past me and looks up.

—Yes, I see him too, she says.

I look at the windows on the second and third floors, but can see nothing. Why should he be there anyhow when it's No. 75? They were pulling my leg.